GRUENE GENERAL STORE COOKBOOK

Tried and True Recipes from the Heart of the Hill Country

By Virginia Keys Hughes

First Printing, June 1998, 5,000 copies
Second Printing, November 1999, 7,500 copies

Copyright © 1998 Hughes Interests

Published by
Hughes Interests
5325 River Oaks Drive
New Braunfels, Texas 78132

ISBN: 0-9664328-0-0

Photography of Gruene in its early days
courtesy of Kyle and Ethelene Gruene

Reproduction sign images printed with
permission by Harvey's Wallhangers

cookbook
resources.
541 Doubletree Drive
Highland Village, Texas 75067
972/317-0245

CONTENTS

★

A NOTE FROM THE AUTHOR

★

Just mention the Hill Country of Texas, and a wistful, faraway look comes into the eye; those who are familiar with the lakes, rivers, hills and wildflowers of the heart of the state long for the opportunity to live in small towns like New Braunfels or others near to it. The historical hamlet of Gruene especially seems to appeal to those who are familiar with it by virtue of being able to spend vacations or long weekends in the area, soaking up its German and Mexican heritage and indulging in a little toe-tapping in Gruene Hall or strolling the shops of Gruene.

No matter where one grew up, everyone remembers "home", and those memories almost always include fond recollections of food, family meals, and happy times around the dinner table. I grew up in the oil patch of Arkansas, the child of a Louisiana Cajun mother and a father who came from a long line of Southerners. My cooking has been heavily influenced by my grandmothers and my mother, all good cooks, and by growing up in a small town where the word "vegetables" was synonymous with good eating.

My paternal grandmother, "Miss Fannie" Keys, ran a school cafeteria in the days when a dietician's degree wasn't necessary to hold down that job; you just needed to know how to cook and how to manage the help. My maternal grandmother, Lena Robin Mistrot, cooked everything with onion, garlic and bell pepper, and "rice" was the only four-letter word she ever knew. My mother, Evelyn Mistrot Keys, widowed at the age of 41, not only worked outside the home and raised three children by herself; she also cooked three meals a day! And finally, my daughter, Angela Dickerson Noble, has carried on the tradition of good cooking by introducing me to many delicious innovative vegetarian recipes and ways of cooking for the new generation.

In this book of recipes, some of which are mine but many of which have been contributed by family and friends, I've attempted to bring together the best of the old and new, in a particular effort to evoke the atmosphere of the Central Texas hill country which has been my home now for many years. The German recipes, so familiar to those whose heritage lies in that generation of brave immigrants who settled this country; the recipes contributed by family and friends; the tasty "new cuisine"foods which reflect our interest in low fat, healthy alternatives— all these combine, I hope, to present to the reader a collection of recipes that will become the source of good eating for friends and family.

My many thanks to James Williamson for his research on Gruene and to all the contributors in helping me compile this treasury of home cooking. A special thank you to my husband, Gordon, who encouraged me to write this book and who never fails to appreciate my cooking, and who also never fails to say "thank you for the nice dinner". As any cook will agree, appreciation sweetens the pot!

Guten Appetit,
Virginia Keys Hughes

HOW THE GRUENE GENERAL STORE CAME TO BE

★

In 1876 Henry D. Gruene established his farming empire on the banks of the Guadalupe, raising cotton on land extending all the way from New Braunfels to San Marcos, including the little town of Hunter, for which Hunter Road is named. He opened a company store to service his employees and family members, all of whom held positions in his farming business and all of whom who lived and raised their families in the little settlement where they

This early photo of the Gruene General Store depicts the agriculture-centered lifestyle of the area. The wagons with their loads of cotton bales were headed for the cotton gin in Gruene. Cotton was the principal cash crop of the Gruene family operation before the cotton boll weevil ruined the business.

lived. The Gruene General Store sold all the necessities for families of that time; sugar, flour and meal, fabric for the ladies' dresses, farm equipment and hardware for the sharecropper's needs. Henry liked to say that he sold "everything from coffins to real estate".

Henry D. Gruene, his grandson Jim Ogletree, employees of the Gruene family enterprises and even Spot, the dog are pictured here in front of Gruene Hall in a photograph taken about 1910.

As the little community grew, the store became too small and so, in the German tradition of frugality, Henry Gruene moved the frame building across the street and built a larger brick building for his mercantile business. The frame building became several other entities under the Gruene family business but then was closed and vacant for many years.

Antique store fixtures such as this rack for handled implements are typical of the authentic touches found in the Gruene General Store.

In March of 1989, the original Gruene General Store, now refurbished and fitted out with antique fixtures, re-opened. Gordon and Virginia Hughes set out to make the new Gruene General Store as versatile and unique as old Mr. Gruene's store had been. The store doesn't sell coffins, and it doesn't sell real estate, but it sells just about everything else! The Gruene General Store specializes in an extensive selection of Texas-made food products, souvenirs and gifts, gourmet coffees, antique advertising signs and memorabilia, and Texas music, available in cassette or CD. The old-fashioned soda fountain features hand-dipped Blue Bell ice cream, homemade fudge, soft drinks, and candy-by-the-pound. A specialty is the 5 cent cup of coffee, a bargain not to be found anywhere else in recent memory! Today the store carries over 10,000 different items, so come see for yourself! The Schindler family, who now own and operate the store, are carrying on the tradition of "something for everyone".

The Gruene General Store has been featured in numerous television commercials and has been the subject of travelogues and newspaper articles in many newspapers. We think the reason it's such a popular place is that it truly appeals to everyone. Men, women and children like it. Young people and old people like it. It has humor (sometimes a little off the wall), but it pokes fun at everyone, and all in fun.

The Gruene General Store is open every day of the year, except for Christmas Day and Thanksgiving Day. Our phone number is (830) 629-6021. Any of the merchandise sold in the Gruene General Store can be ordered by telephone, so give us a call.

A BRIEF HISTORY OF GRUENE

★

T he history of Gruene the town is, more or less, the history of Gruene the man. Henry Gruene, the son of German immigrants and a strong-willed and able-minded man, founded the town as a young man and two lived and prospered together.

In the spring of 1870, Henry Gruene was a 19 year old boy itching for a change. It was an itch he

Henry Gruene's general store, established 1876, was an important community center in the early years of the 20th century. Customers came from miles around to shop at Mr. Gruene's store. H.D. Gruene boasted that he sold "everything from coffins to real estate".

must have inherited. Twenty years earlier his parents had come from Germany to the newly independent Republic of Texas, searching for the prosperity and freedom that so many German immigrants had come to find.

In this photograph from the 1930's, Gruene's Fire Department truck was proudly on display. Note the dirt roads and now defunct John Deere tractor dealership at the corner of Hunter Road and Gruene Road. Except for new signage, this corner in Gruene looks remarkably the same today.

Henry's parents had settled down as farmers near the German settlement called New Braunfels, but Henry was looking for something more glamorous. So that spring Henry and three friends decided to try cowboy life, signing on to drive a herd to Utah. De-

Shown before its extensive renovation, the old cotton gin building now known as the Gristmill Restaurant is a popular riverfront destination for both area residents and visitors to Gruene. Additions in an authentic matching style include large dining rooms and a multi-tiered deck arranged to take advantage of the Guadalupe River views. Diners may choose open-air seating or may dine in air-conditioned comfort in its new dining area.

spite bad weather, lonely nights, and a strong desire to go home, they finished the drive. When a second drive ended with a bankrupt buyer and no payment for 335 head of cattle, Henry decided to retire from cowboy life, find a wife, and take up farming.

The large tract of land on the east bank of the Guadalupe River, a few miles northeast of New Braunfels, that Henry and his new wife Bertha settled on was destined to be more than just another farm. The land Henry had chosen was flat and fertile, ideal for farming, so when he offered to rent plots of land for sharecropping, families came from all over to take him up on the offer. Within a few months Gruene was renting land to twenty to thirty families, each of whom got 100 to 200 acres to farm. Almost in the blink of an eye Henry Gruene, recently retired cowboy and newlywed farmer, had founded his own town: Gruene, Texas.

The town continued to grow as Henry's sharecropping system prospered and in 1878 he established the Gruene General Store. Local farmers would buy what they needed on credit and then pay the store back after the harvest. The general store was followed quickly by a cotton gin to process the most popular cash crop among

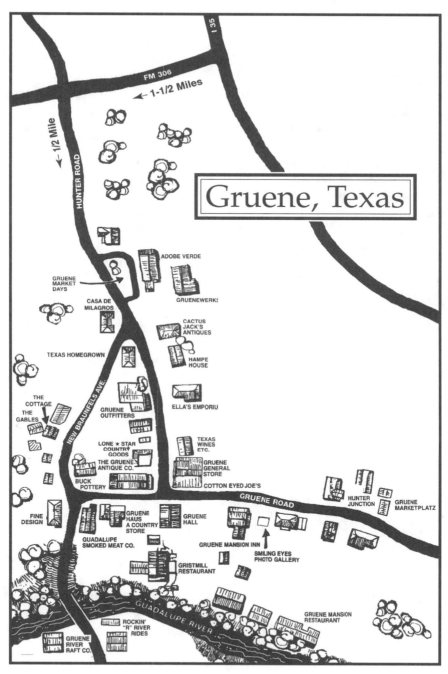

A map of Gruene, Texas shows its proximity to Interstate 35 and the Guadalupe River. The river was an important amenity to early settlers as the cotton gin was water-powered.

local farmers. Near the gin Gruene established a lumber yard...a lucrative business in a region where it was tradition for fathers to build houses for each of their children as they married and started their families.

In addition to his rapidly growing commercial interests, Gruene also took a fatherly interest in the welfare and happiness of his tenant farmers, treating them almost like an extended family. 1874 saw the construction of a school for educating the local children. For the adults, Gruene established an amusement hall consisting then, as now, of a dance hall and tavern, where the locals would bring their families and dance from early Saturday evening till five o'clock Sunday morning, just in time to get ready for church.

Gruene was a family town; Henry's continued prosperity was the town's as well. By the time Henry retired in 1910, the town had a blacksmith shop, two railroad depots, a post office, and a second mercantile with business that rivaled anything in nearby New Braunfels.

In 1925 the boll weevil so devastated crops that not a single bale of cotton was saved. Just as farmers began to recover, the Great Depression struck. Tenant farmers sank farther and farther into debt, taking down with them the general store that depended on their business. The increased mobility brought on by the automobile also played a part in the demise of the once-thriving community, giving locals the ability to seek work and buy merchandise at cheaper prices in New Braunfels. Cheaper and better cotton being grown in south Texas made cotton farming a losing proposition. Within a few years the railroads had left, the highway had moved, and the post office had been closed down. Gruene, Texas was a ghost town. Only the dance hall remained open and viable, still patronized by the local people as a familiar source of entertainment.

In 1974 some developers purchased the town and the land around it with the intention of razing the buildings and constructing a subdivision. Lovers of Texas history intervened, and in 1975 the State Historical Commission declared the area an Historic District. With an almost unprecedented show of unanimity, the group of people who now own the buildings have committed to preserving the architectural integrity of Gruene.

GOOD BEGINNINGS

Welcoming the visitor to Gruene, Texas at the top of the hill leading up from the Guadalupe River, this sign marks the first glimpse of the historic district with its buildings reminiscent of the vernacular style of Texas architecture prominent in the late 19th and early 20th century.

"Gruene's" Hall was the entertainment center for the local population in the early 1900's. Many a romance began on the old dance floor. In its heyday it hosted local bands as well as up-and-coming young bandleaders such as Lawrence Welk. Today it continues as a popular local and regional dance hall.

Gruene Hall pictured today is the recipient of a Texas Historical Medallion. Billed as the "oldest dance hall in Texas", it is the venue for well known performers such as Jerry Jeff Walker, Ray Price, Buddy Guy, Robert Earl Keene, Leon Russell, and Hal Ketchum. Local bands play here, too, with live performances Thursday through Sunday during most of the year, and every night during the summer season. The front part of the hall, where local performers play on Sunday afternoons, has the original bar and a

wood-burning stove which feels mighty good on cold winter days and nights. Games of cards or dominoes are brought out while the bands are taking breaks, and babies and children play while their parents or grandparents enjoy the music, games or conversation. The dance floor is made up of wide old boards which have

Young members of the Henry Gruene family are pictured on the mansion porch in this photograph from about 1910. Jim Ogletree, grandson of H.D. Gruene, is at left. Note the extensive landscaping in the yard. Below, the Gruene Mansion Inn as pictured today. Now a popular bed-and-breakfast, units in the rear overlook the Guadalupe River. Breakfast in the Gruene Mansion Inn dining room is a treat to be savored. The Gruene Mansion Inn Restaurant, also overlooking the river, is located on the grounds.

hosted many dancing feet over the years. Authentic local advertising signs from the days when telephone numbers had no prefix line the rafters. Off to the side, pool tables are used by young and old alike, and out in the adjacent beergarten a game of horseshoes is likely to be going on.

Henry Gruene built his hall as an entertainment center for his family, employees, and their children back in the days when good company was scarce and socializing was a luxury; today Gruene Hall carries on the tradition of being a place where "just folks" can get together for a good time.

PARTY FOODS
PARTY PLANNING CHART

I have used this chart, which I cut out of a magazine years ago, many times. I find that guests do not eat nearly as much as you think they will, especially at a cocktail party or open house. They are usually more interested in talking or drinking than they are in eating! The following list of amounts of food and beverages is for 25 cocktail buffet guests.

Hors d'oeuvres—3$^{1}/_{2}$ per person (includes finger sandwiches)

Olives, carrot and celery sticks, etc.—2 each per person

Dips—1 cup serves 10 people if served with crackers or chips that pick up heavily; more if served with chips that tend to crumble.

Chips, snack crackers, etc.—1 of the largest size bags of potato chips plus 1 of the largest size bags of corn or tortilla chips.

Cheese—1 pound, very thinly sliced

Meats—2 pounds very thinly sliced ham, turkey, or cold cuts

Nuts—2 pounds

Pick-up desserts, such as tartlets, petit fours—1 per person

Champagne—One bottle ($^{4}/_{5}$ quart) makes 8 servings.

Wine—One bottle ($^{4}/_{5}$ quart) makes 5 medium size glasses. One case (12 bottles) will make 60 medium size glasses.

Punch—Four gallons will make 100 (5 ounce) servings, or about 20 cups per gallon.

Alcoholic drinks—Each person will have 2 to 3 drinks. If you are entertaining 12 people, you will need 2 or 3 fifths; for 25 people, 5 or 6 fifths, etc.

TEXAS CAVIAR BALLS O' FIRE

These little morsels are always a hit with the men!

1 jar D. L. Jardine's Texas Caviar (jalapeno-stuffed olives)
2 cups grated cheddar cheese
¹/₂ cup butter (not margarine)
1 cup flour
1 teaspoon salt
1 teaspoon cayenne pepper
1 cup finely chopped pecans or
1 cup crushed Rice Krispies

Preheat oven to 375 degrees. Blend cheese and butter together. Sift flour with salt and cayenne pepper. Work flour mixture into cheese mixture. Add nuts or Rice Krispies. Use one tablespoon of dough to cover one jalapeno-stuffed olive. Insert the jalapeno-stuffed olive into the dough. Cover the olive with the dough by rolling the dough and olive between the palms of your hands. Place on cookie sheet and bake at 375 degrees until golden brown.

JARDINE FOODS OF TEXAS

A parking lot now takes the place of the Gruene Brothers Lumber Company building shown here in this 1940's photograph. The dirt roads have been replaced with paving, but much of the town of Gruene remains the same as in the early 20th century.

ANGELA'S ORIGINAL
RED OR GREEN SALSA

My daughter, Angela, is a fine cook. She made up this recipe one day and it has become a family favorite.

10 large ripe Roma tomatoes or 1 1/2 pounds tomatillos, husked but not cooked
1 bunch cilantro
1 large onion
1 large jalapeno
2 tablespoons lime juice
1 tablespoon white vinegar
5 cloves garlic
2 tablespoons salt
2 teaspoons black pepper

Chop vegetables where necessary. Place in blender or food processor and purée. Serve with tortilla chips. This is better the second day, after flavors have more time to mingle! Keeps well in refrigerator.

ANGELA D. NOBLE

CORN-TOMATO SALSA

Good with chips as a dip or as an accompaniment to chicken or pinto beans.

1 tomato, chopped
1 cup corn, cooked (canned or frozen)
1 clove garlic, mashed in mortar or press
¹/₄ teaspoon onion powder
1 cup cilantro, chopped
2 chiles, chopped
Juice of 1 lime

Mix all together and chill for several hours to allow flavors to blend.

PARTY CHEESE BALL

This recipe comes from Tammy's mother-in-law. It makes a great party dish.
All ingredients should be at room temperature.

2 (8 ounce) packages cream cheese
2 (5 ounce) jars Old English cheese
1 jar Roka Blue Cheese or 4 ounces Blue Cheese
2 or 3 green onions (chopped fine)
Chopped pecans
Chopped parsley
1 clove garlic

Rub garlic clove around inside of bowl. Mix all ingredients together and form into a ball. Roll cheese ball in chopped pecans and chopped parsley. Refrigerate before serving. Serve with any crackers or chips.

TAMMY HUNTER

ELENORA'S CHEESE BALL

2 (8 ounce) packages cream cheese
4 packages dried beef, cut into very small pieces
    (Carl Buddig Beef Brand)
4 stalks green onion, finely chopped
I teaspoon Worcestershire Sauce
I teaspoon Accent

Soften cream cheese. Add 3 packages dried beef, chopped onion and seasonings and mix well. Shape into ball and roll ball in additional chopped beef. Refrigerate. Serve with crackers.

ELENORA KOHLENBERG

ROTEL, VELVEETA AND THEN SOME

Karen's daughter's mother-in-law from Indiana expanded on an old Texas recipe, and it is really good. This is also wonderful on baked potatoes, steak, etc.

I pound Velveeta
I can chopped Rotel tomatoes (Try the new HOT
    flavor for a real Texas touch)
I package frozen spinach
I can artichoke hearts

Cube Velveeta. Place it in microwave-safe bowl. Add Rotel, chopped artichoke hearts and spinach that has been thawed and drained well. Microwave on high 2 minutes at a time until melted, and stir to mix all ingredients together.

KAREN HOWELL

BACON-WRAPPED CRACKERS

*These tasty bites can be assembled ahead of time
and then baked just before guests arrive.*

12 slices bacon, cut in half
24 saltine crackers

Wrap a half slice of bacon around each cracker, overlapping ends. Place, seam side down, on a rack in a shallow roasting pan; bake at 350 degrees for 30 minutes or until bacon is crisp. Serve immediately. Yield: 2 dozen.

★

COCKTAIL SAUSAGE BALLS

*Whenever we have a party, I always make up a double recipe of
these. They are even good the next day, reheated briefly.*

1 pound hot bulk sausage, uncooked
3 cups biscuit mix
1 pound sharp Cheddar cheese, grated
2 to 4 tablespoons ice water, as needed

Combine sausage, biscuit mix and grated cheese. Add ice water, spoonful by spoonful, as needed to make dough stick together. Shape into cocktail size meatballs. Place on rack in baking pan and bake at 300 degrees until lightly brown, about 25 minutes. These freeze well. Freeze after cooking. Reheat at 350 degrees.

SWEET AND SOUR MEATBALLS

2 pounds ground beef
I cup onion, chopped fine
I cup breadcrumbs
I egg, beaten
I (8 ounce) jar grape jelly
8 ounces catsup
Salt and pepper to taste

Mix the ground beef, onion, breadcrumbs, salt and pepper, and egg. Make into 1-inch meatballs. Place the meatballs on a broiler pan which has been sprayed with cooking spray. Bake at 450 degrees about 25 minutes until brown and done. Drain on paper towels. In a saucepan, heat the catsup and grape jelly until blended and hot. Add the meatballs. Transfer to chafing dish or fondue pot to serve, providing toothpicks to dip the meatballs into the sauce.

SHRIMP DIP

This rich dip is also good as a spread on crackers, and I have even served it as a shrimp salad over sliced tomatoes. It is very rich, so a little goes a long way. This serves 4 as a luncheon salad.

I pound boiled shrimp, finely chopped
I (8 ounce) package cream cheese
4 tablespoons sour cream
I tablespoon each minced onion, parsley, bell pepper, celery, green olives
Cayenne and salt to taste
Mayonnaise to thin

Soften cheese; add other ingredients and mix well. Chill to blend. Best made a day ahead. Serves 20.

BROCCOLI DIP

This may be served hot in a chafing dish or at room temperature. If any is left over (there won't be!) it's good as a topping for baked potatoes.

1/2 **cup onion**
1/2 **cup celery**
1/2 **cup mushrooms**
3 **tablespoons butter**
1 **can cream of mushroom soup**
1 **roll garlic cheese**
1 **package chopped broccoli, cooked and drained**
1 **tablespoon lemon juice**

Sauté onions, celery and mushrooms in butter. Add soup, cheese, broccoli and lemon juice. Stir to blend. Freezes well. Serves 12.

SMOKED PECANS

These are wonderful for a holiday party or anytime. The pecans also make a nice addition to a green salad.

2 **cups pecans**
1 **bottle liquid smoke**

Soak pecans in liquid smoke for 20 minutes. Drain well. Toast in 250 degree oven for 20 minutes. Put 1 teaspoon salt and 1 stick melted butter in jar and shake with pecans. Keep tightly covered.

You can't turn back the clock
but you can wind it up again.

PARTY MOUSSE

This is so easy and dependably good. The mold holds its shape well, so will last for several hours on the buffet table without melting.

1 cup cottage cheese
1 cup sour cream
1 tablespoon Lawry's seasoned salt
1 tablespoon soy sauce
Juice of ¹/₂ lemon
Dash of Tabasco
¹/₄ teaspoon garlic powder
1 ¹/₂ tablespoons gelatin
2 tablespoons sherry or vermouth

Dissolve gelatin in sherry over hot water. Combine other ingredients in a blender or food processor and blend for about one minute. Add gelatin mixture and blend again. Pour into lightly greased mold and chill. Unmold and serve with crackers.

★

SHRIMP MOLD

1 can tomato soup (undiluted)
1 small package Knox unflavored gelatin
1 (8 ounce) package cream cheese, broken into pieces
2 (4 ounce) cans of tiny shrimp, rinsed and drained
³/₄ cup finely chopped celery
¹/₄ cup finely chopped onion
1 cup mayonnaise

Bring soup to a boil. Add gelatin and whisk until dissolved. Remove from heat. Add the rest of the ingredients, except mayonnaise, blending thoroughly. Add mayonnaise, using wire whisk to combine. Pour into mold (a fish-shaped mold is really pretty) and refrigerate overnight. Serve with crackers. Rich and delicious!

MELANIE QUINN

STUFFED MUSHROOMS

This recipe is great for those who remember when "hors d'ouevres"
meant something besides cheese and crackers. Delicious!

1 pound large fresh mushrooms
2 or 3 green onions, chopped, tops and all
1 rib celery, finely chopped
Stems from mushrooms, finely chopped
$^1/_4$ to $^1/_2$ cup Progresso breadcrumbs
1 to 2 tablespoons white wine
$^1/_2$ teaspoon salt
$^1/_4$ teaspoon red pepper
12 tablespoons butter

Wash mushrooms; remove stems for use in the filling. Sauté vegetables in butter, add breadcrumbs and seasonings. Add wine and mix until a dressing-like consistency is obtained. Fill mushroom caps with the dressing mixture. Arrange on a greased baking sheet and bake at 350 degrees for 15 to 20 minutes.

RASPBERRY CHIPOTLE/CREAM CHEESE HORS D'OEUVRES

This is a new variation on the old standby of jalapeno jelly served over cream cheese. Fischer & Weiser's Roasted Raspberry Chipotle Sauce received Outstanding New Best-Seller 1997 award from the National Association of Specialty Foods Trade! It's delicious and is available at the Gruene General Store!

1 (8 ounce) package cream cheese
1 bottle Fischer & Wieser Roasted Raspberry Chipotle Sauce
Crackers

Place cream cheese on plate. Pour sauce over cream cheese. Serve with crackers.

FISCHER & WIESER SPECIALTY FOODS
FREDERICKSBURG, TEXAS

PAMPELL'S CHOCOLATE ICE CREAM SODA

Pampell's Drugstore in Kerrville specializes in old-fashioned soda fountain treats.

1 scoop vanilla ice cream
3 tablespoons chocolate syrup
Spray of carbonated water

Blend by hand all of the above into a thick paste. Fill soda glass ³/₄ full with carbonated water. Float 2 scoops of vanilla ice cream on top. Carbonate briefly again and serve. Makes one serving.

SANDY AND JON WOLFMUELLER
PAMPELL'S DRUGSTORE
KERRVILLE, TEXAS

★

PAMPELL'S PUNCH

Juice from ¹/₂ lemon
Juice from ¹/₂ lime
2 teaspoons cherry syrup
2 tablespoons simple syrup (1:1 sugar and water)

Mix with plain or carbonated water. Add ice and a cherry. Garnish with lemon and/or lime slices. Makes one serving.

SANDY AND JON WOLFMUELLER
PAMPELL'S DRUGSTORE
KERRVILLE, TEXAS

PERCOLATOR PUNCH

2 (32 ounce) bottles cranberry juice
1 (46 ounce) can pineapple juice
1 cup brown sugar
4 teaspoons whole cloves
Peel from ¼ orange, cut in strips
12-inch cinnamon stick, broken
1 fifth light rum (optional)

Mix the juices and brown sugar together. Put liquid into a 24-cup coffee percolator. Put the cloves, cinnamon stick and orange peel into the basket, and perk. Makes 17 cups.

BOURBON SLUSH

Growing up in a rural area which was also "dry", about the only time our family drank alcohol was at holiday time. My uncle Robert was the Tax Collector and Assessor of Union County, and he was pretty dependable about furnishing the liquor for family gatherings. There was something deliciously dangerous about having a holiday toddy in a dry county, especially if it was in my grandmother's house!

1 (12 ounce) can frozen orange juice
1 (12 ounce) can frozen lemonade
2 cups sugar
2 cups strong tea (made with 3 bags)
7 cups hot water
2 cups bourbon

Make tea with 2 cups water and 3 tea bags. Dissolve sugar in 7 cups hot water. Add other ingredients. Freeze in 13 x 9-inch pan. To serve, chop up coarsely and fill glasses. Add 7-Up, Perrier water, or club soda to fill the glasses. Makes 20 drinks.

CRANBERRY SLUSH

This is a soft-serve drink and when mixed with the 7-Up is the consistency of a daiquiri. This can also be made without the vodka for a treat the whole family can enjoy. This recipe has made the rounds of our entire family. Delicious!

2 quarts cranberry juice
¹/₂ cup sugar
¹/₂ cup water
I small can orange juice concentrate
I small can lemonade concentrate
I cup vodka (optional)

Dissolve sugar in water over heat. Add juices. Mix with rest of ingredients. Freeze in Tupperware container. Mix with 7-Up to serve.

JILL KNEUPER

BLOODY MARIA

3 parts D. L. Jardine's Red Snapper Bloody Mary Mix
I part tequila
3 to 4 D. L. Jardine's Texas Caviar (jalapeno-stuffed olives)
Ice

Combine Red Snapper and tequila. Pour into serving glasses over ice. Garnish with olives and a twist of lime, if desired.

JARDINE FOODS OF TEXAS

COLD SPICED COFFEE

Aspen Mulling Spice is available at the Gruene General Store.

Place 2 tablespoons Aspen Mulling Spices on top of ground coffee in brewing basket of your coffee maker. Brew coffee. Pour spiced coffee mixture into an ice cube tray and freeze. Add spiced coffee ice cubes to regular coffee to give it a subtle spiciness.

ASPEN MULLING SPICES
ASPEN, COLORADO

★

TEXAS TEA

Only in Texas, home of Dr. Pepper, but this is really good!

1 (12 ounce) Dr. Pepper, heated
1 teaspoon Aspen Mulling Spice

Mix Dr. Pepper and mulling spice until spice is dissolved. Serves 1.

ASPEN MULLING SPICE
ASPEN, COLORADO

★

RUSSIAN TEA

5 quarts prepared tea (regular or herbal)
Juice of 6 oranges
Juice of 6 lemons
1 carton Aspen Mulling Spice

Heat tea, orange juice and lemon juice just until hot—do not boil. Remove from heat. Stir in Aspen Mulling Spices. Serve hot.

ASPEN MULLING SPICE
ASPEN, COLORADO

HOT SPICED TEA MIX

*This was a very popular recipe during the 60's
and 70's, and still is a good one to know.*

1 cup (1 ounce) instant tea
2 cups (18 ounce jar) Tang
¹/₂ cup sugar
1 (30 ounce) package lemonade mix
2 teaspoons cinnamon
1 teaspoon cloves

Sift together thoroughly. Add 2 or 3 spoonsful to a cup of very hot
water to make a single serving.

TANTIE'S HOT TODDY

*If you have a cold or the flu, just before going to bed
at night mix up this concoction and sip slowly. It will
surely make you sleep well and wake up feeling better.*

Juice of 1 lemon
2 tablespoons sugar
¹/₄ cup rum or bourbon
Boiling water

Mix lemon, sugar and rum or bourbon together in mug. Fill with
boiling water and stir. Sip and enjoy.

ASPEN HOLIDAY WASSAIL

1 gallon apple cider
1 (46 ounce) can pineapple juice
1 (6 ounce) can frozen orange juice
1 carton Aspen Mulling Spice
6 cinnamon sticks
1 apple, cut into rings
2 oranges, cut into rings

Heat cider, juices and cinnamon sticks together in large container (can be done in 30 cup electric percolator). Simmer to let flavors blend. Pour into punch bowl to serve. For garnish, put apples and oranges on cinnamon sticks and float on top of the wassail.

═══════ ★ ═══════

WASSAIL

1 gallon apple cider
1 quart orange juice
1 cup lemon juice
1 large can pineapple juice
24 whole cloves
1 cup granulated sugar
4 sticks cinnamon

Combine the juices and sugar in a large saucepan. Put the cloves and cinnamon in a muslin bag and place in the saucepan while bringing to a boil. Simmer 5 or 10 minutes. Makes 1 1/2 gallons.

EAT YOUR VEGETABLES

Vegetables, condiments and salsas, and other home-grown treats await the visitor to the Gruene General Store. A veritable bounty of good stuff to eat, including old-fashioned dill pickles and pickled peaches, is found on its authentic shelving and displays.

G ruene's red brick mercantile store, built in the early 1900's, replaced the original wooden building constructed on this site. The store featured a bank vault and a post office as well as a full basement. Here Mr. Gruene displayed merchandise his sharecroppers needed to make their lives a little easier. In addition to staples like flour and sugar and farm implements, the store carried fabric for the ladies' dresses, penny candy for the children, and of course a few treats for the gents, like tobacco and "Green River Whiskey", Henry Gruene's own brand of liquor which was distributed from the location.

In the interior shot of the store, a banner from Depression days informs customers "We sell for cash only", bringing to an end the era of family charge accounts which could be settled when the cotton crop came in. Hard times brought the closing of the mercantile store in the mid-1930's.

The water tower in

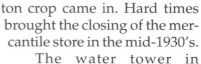

Gruene is its landmark and symbol; a reminder of a more relaxed, simpler way of life when people relied on themselves and their neighbors to create a community where they worked, lived, and played in harmony, trust and peace. The planned demolition of the water tower in the early 1970's to make way for a housing development was the catalyst for the revival of Gruene, which had become a ghost town.

TOMATO BASIL SOUP

This is one of Huisache Grill's most popular soups.

8 fresh ripe tomatoes, stems removed and quartered
2 tablespoons chopped fresh basil
I can diced red peppers
I (12 ounce) can tomato sauce
2 cloves fresh garlic
Pinch white pepper
Pinch red pepper flakes
Salt to taste

In a food processor, combine all above ingredients and blend well. Cook over medium heat in a heavy saucepan 20 to 30 minutes.

Garnish: Croutons - baked rounds of French bread brushed with olive oil and sprinkled with more chopped basil. Sprinkle grated Romano cheese on top and serve.

Huisache Grill
New Braunfels, Texas

TORTILLA SOUP

Tortilla soup is practically a staple in Texas. This recipe makes a nice first course or can be served as the main dish for a soup supper.

4 quarts chicken broth
5 or 6 chicken breasts
3 cans Rotel Chiles and Tomatoes
2 cups chopped yellow onions
3 tablespoons chopped cilantro
3 tablespoons chili powder
3 tablespoons cumin
3 tablespoons garlic powder
Garnish: shredded Monterey Jack cheese
Green onion
Sour cream
Tortilla chips
Sliced avocado

Place chicken in broth, bring to a boil and simmer one hour, until chicken is done. Add Rotel tomatoes, onions, cilantro, chili powder, cumin and garlic powder; cook for an additional hour. Chicken should shred apart and onions should be translucent. In each bowl, ladle 1 cup of soup and top with crumbled tortilla chips. Sprinkle green onions and Monterey Jack cheese on top. Dollop sour cream on top, place avocado slices on either side. Garnish with sprig of cilantro and lime wedge.

GRISTMILL RESTAURANT
GRUENE TEXAS

Use it up, wear it out, make it do, do without
—Depression era motto

ARMANDO'S TORTILLA SOUP

For all those who think tortilla soup is too hard to make, here is YOUR recipe!
This recipe can be multiplied by the number of servings needed.

¹/₄ cup mozzarella cheese, shredded
8 ounces chicken stock
1 ounce (about 2 tablespoons) diced avocado
1 ounce mild red salsa
Broken tortilla chips
2 tablespoons cooked rice
Chopped cilantro

For extra flavor, cook rice in additional chicken stock instead of water. Have all ingredients ready. Heat the 8 ounces of stock with the salsa. In a soup bowl, place rice, cheese and diced avocado. Add stock and salsa. Sprinkle chips and cilantro on top. Makes 1 bowl.

STEAK SOUP

1 stick margarine or butter
1 cup flour
1 pound ground beef
1 cup chopped celery
1 cup onion chunks
1 cup sliced carrots
1 ½ cups frozen mixed vegetables
1 (18 ounce) can tomatoes, chopped (reserve tomato
    juice for use as "liquid")
5 cups liquid (tomato juice, bouillon, water)
1 ½ teaspoons Kitchen Bouquet
5 beef bouillon cubes, dissolved in one cup of the "liquid"
1 tablespoon black pepper, freshly ground

Brown meat and drain. Chop tomatoes and set aside. Melt margarine in large pot on medium-high heat. Whip in flour to make a smooth paste (roux). Add liquids (bouillon first) gradually, stirring to remove lumps. Continue stirring as roux thickens. Add pepper and tomatoes and cook a few minutes. Add Kitchen Bouquet, vegetables and cooked beef. Stir to mix. Cook over medium heat for 30 minutes, stirring occasionally. DO NOT SALT. Makes 2 quarts, and may be frozen for later use.

MELANIE QUINN

No one who cooks cooks alone. Even at her most solitary, a cook in the kitchen is surrounded by generations of cooks past, the advice and menus of cooks present, the wisdom of cookbook writers.

—Laurie Colwin

MEXICAN BEAN SOUP

My sister-in-law, Jody, says she probably got this recipe from a magazine years ago, and has never met anyone yet who didn't ask her for the recipe after being served the soup. It's quick, easy and delicious, and her favorite wintertime soup! For a nice holiday gift, put all the ingredients in a basket with the recipe and tie with a pretty ribbon.

4 slices bacon, diced
³/₄ cup chopped onion
³/₄ cup chopped celery
I clove garlic, minced
I (4 ounce) can chopped green chilies
I (16 ounce) can refried beans
¹/₄ teaspoon black pepper
¹/₄ teaspoon chili powder
I (13 ¹/₂ ounce) can chicken broth
Shredded cheese
Tortilla chips

In a 2 quart saucepan, cook bacon until crisp. Add onion, celery and garlic. Cover and cook over low heat, stirring occasionally, for 10 minutes. Add green chilies, beans, pepper and chili powder. Stir in chicken broth; combine thoroughly. Bring to a boil. Serve in bowls over tortilla chips. Sprinkle cheese and broken chips on top. Makes 5 one-cup servings.

JODY HODGES

The difference between cats and dogs:
a dog comes when called; a cat takes a
message and gets back to you.

DALLAS COUNTY JAILHOUSE CHILI

This is my brother George's recipe which he submitted to me. The recipe is printed just the way he wrote it, so be sure to read it all the way through. He lives in Hawaii and has made that trip many times.

2 pounds diced stew beef
1 teaspoon white pepper
1 tablespoon cumin
3 cups water
1 ¹/₂ tablespoons paprika
3 cloves chopped garlic
1 tablespoon salt
3 tablespoons chili powder

Put a little oil in a crock pot, then add all ingredients and let cook all day. Stir occasionally. Adjust water to desired consistency. Meat will flake easily when done. This recipe is from a Braniff Airlines magazine I read once on my frequent trips between Honolulu and Dallas on Fat Albert, the orange 747 that flew that route. The original recipe called for melting ¹/₂ pound ground beef suet in the pot first, also for 1 ¹/₂ tablespoons diced sweet pepper pods, but those weren't available in Hawaii, so they were omitted. You may have to experiment with cook time and temperature, as crock pots vary. This is not a hot Texas chili, but is very tasty and I like it over rice. Besides, my sister wrote this book!

GEORGE KEYS

McILHENNY'S CHILI

McIlhenny's Tabasco pepper sauce can be found at the Gruene General Store, along with several of their other products.

¹/₄ cup vegetable oil
3 pounds lean beef chuck, well-trimmed,
 cut into 1-inch squares
1 cup onion, chopped
3 cloves garlic, minced
3 tablespoons chili powder
2 teaspoons ground cumin
2 teaspoons salt
2 teaspoons Tabasco pepper sauce
3 cups water
1 (4 ounce) can chopped green chilies, drained
Hot cooked rice

In 5-quart Dutch oven or saucepot heat oil over medium-high heat. Add beef, ¹/₃ at a time; cook until browned on all sides. Remove; set aside. Add onion and garlic; stirring frequently, cook 5 minutes or until tender. Stir in chili powder, cumin, salt and Tabasco sauce; cook 1 minute. Add water and chilies; bring to a boil. Return beef to Dutch oven. Reduce heat and simmer 1¹/₂ hours or until beef is tender. Serve over rice with chopped onion, shredded cheese and sour cream, if desired. Makes 4 to 6 servings.

McIlhenny Company
Tabasco Brand Products

JOHNNY CACE'S GUMBO

Johnny Cace grew up in South Louisiana. He has wonderful restaurants in San Antonio, Tyler, and Longview, Texas. This is one of the recipes brought from South Louisiana.

1 cup onions
3 cloves garlic, chopped
4 tablespoons flour
$^1/_2$ cup tomato paste
1 #2 can of tomatoes
2 pounds small shrimp
2 quarts water
1 tablespoon gumbo filé
2 bay leaves
Pinch of thyme
Dash of Accent
1 cup chopped celery
2 tablespoons parsley
1 cup crabmeat
Salt and pepper to taste

To make roux, brown 4 tablespoons flour in $^1/_2$ cup oil, stirring constantly. Sauté onions and garlic and add to roux. Add tomato paste and tomatoes. Then add water, bay leaves, thyme, Accent, celery, parsley, crabmeat, salt and pepper. Bring to boil and simmer for 1 hour. Add shrimp and cook 20 minutes. Take 1 cup broth out and add filé and stir until dissolved. Return to pot and stir. Pour over cooked rice and enjoy.

PAT FRASE

Nothing in the world can take the place of persistence.

CONNOLLY'S CHICKEN GUMBO

When I lived in Louisiana I had a dear friend from New Orleans who gave me this recipe. She was a wonderful Cajun cook. This is always the way I "finish up" our Thanksgiving turkey scraps. Boil the turkey carcass for the broth.

4 tablespoons oil
4 tablespoons flour
I large onion, chopped fine
3 cloves garlic, minced
I green pepper, chopped fine
3 ribs celery, sliced
I can tomatoes, chopped
2 cups broth or water
2 to 3 cups chicken or turkey, chopped
Salt and pepper to taste
2 bay leaves
File powder
White rice

First you make a roux: in a large, heavy pot heat oil until hot; stir in flour. Cook over medium heat, stirring constantly, for 10 to 12 minutes until very dark brown. Do not let roux burn. Add onion, garlic, pepper and celery and cook until wilted, 5 minutes or so, stirring often so as not to burn. Add tomatoes and juice and water, stirring so as not to lump. Add meat and spices. Simmer for about an hour. (Shrimp or sausage and okra may be added to this if you have some on hand.) When ready to serve, put a mound of rice in bowl and ladle gumbo over. Add about ½ teaspoon file powder to each bowl.

HELPFUL HINT:

The best piece of cooking equipment any cook can own is an iron skillet.

DUCK GUMBO

1 (4 pound) domestic duck, cut up
1 teaspoon Tabasco pepper sauce, divided
Salt
2 tablespoons vegetable oil
2 tablespoons butter or margarine
$^1/_2$ cup celery, chopped
1 cup onion, chopped
1 cup green pepper, chopped
2 cloves garlic, minced
3 tablespoons flour
3 cups chicken broth
24 shucked oysters with liquor
$^1/_4$ cup green onions, sliced
$^1/_4$ cup parsley, chopped
Hot cooked rice

Season duck with $^1/_2$ teaspoon Tabasco sauce; sprinkle with salt. In large deep skillet or Dutch oven, heat oil over medium-high heat. Add duck; brown on all sides. Remove; set aside. Pour off fat. In same skillet, melt butter over medium-high heat. Stir in flour; cook 5 minutes or until a brown roux is formed. Add celery, onion, green pepper and garlic; stirring frequently, cook 5 minutes or until tender. Gradually stir in broth and remaining $^1/_2$ teaspoon Tabasco sauce; cook 5 minutes or until slightly thickened. Return duck to skillet; bring to boil. Cover; reduce heat and simmer 1 hour or until duck is tender. Stir in oysters with liquor, green onions and parsley; cook 10 minutes or until oysters curl. Serve over rice. Makes 4 servings.

McIlhenny Company
Tabasco Brand Products

SOUTHWESTERN CORN CHOWDER

*Don't be discouraged by the long list of ingredients
in this recipe. Once everything has been assembled,
it goes together quickly and is really delicious.*

8 vegetable bouillon cubes
8 cups water
4 medium white potatoes
2 large yellow squash, cubed
16 ounces frozen corn
1 tablespoon honey
2 teaspoons Worcestershire sauce
2 tablespoons butter or margarine
2 tablespoons oil
1 large onion, chopped
1 large bell pepper, diced
3 ribs of celery with leaves, diced
2 tablespoons chili powder
2 teaspoons cumin
3 cloves garlic, pressed
3 tablespoons flour
1 cup milk
1 cup heavy whipping cream
1 jalapeno pepper, sliced
2 tablespoons pickled jalapeno juice
Crumbled tortilla chips

In a large soup pot, bring water to a boil and dissolve bouillon. Add potatoes and let simmer uncovered about 10 minutes. Add squash and continue to simmer until both squash and potatoes are tender. Stir in the corn, honey and Worcestershire. Cover and simmer mixture on low about 20 minutes.

Meanwhile, heat the butter and oil in a medium skillet. Sauté onion until it starts to soften. Add bell pepper and celery and sauté 5 minutes more. Stir in chili powder, cumin and garlic. Turn down heat to medium low. Sprinkle on flour and mix in. Gradually add the milk and cook until thickened, stirring to prevent lumps.

In blender or food processor, purée $1/3$ of the sautéed vegetables, $1/2$ of the potatoes and squash (sans liquid) and the cream. Stir the purée back into the soup along with the remaining sautéed veggies. Add salt, jalapeno, jalapeno juice and black pepper to taste. Allow to cook another 10 minutes or so (DO NOT LET BOIL). Ladle into bowls and garnish with crumbled tortilla chips.

LOW-FAT VERSION: Use skim milk and substitute evaporated skim milk for cream.

NOT-AS-HOT VERSION: Seed the jalapeno or simply omit.

ANGELA D. NOBLE

COWBOY STEW

This recipe came from Jody's mother-in-law, Patricia Hodges.

1 pound ground beef
1 onion
1 bell pepper (optional)
2 cloves garlic
1 (15 ounce) can tomatoes
1 can corn
1 can ranch style beans
3 to 4 potatoes, diced

Brown meat, onion and garlic. Add vegetables. Cook until potatoes are tender. You may have to add a little water. Salt and pepper to taste.

JODY HODGES

FRESH ASPARAGUS-POTATO CREAM SOUP

*This makes a good first course for a dinner party
or is hearty enough for a main dish soup.*

1 bunch (or 1 pound) fresh asparagus
4 large white potatoes, cubed
3 vegetable bouillon cubes
1 medium onion, chopped
4 tablespoons butter or margarine
4 tablespoons flour
2 cups milk
2 teaspoons lemon juice
1 teaspoon dill
1 teaspoon coriander
1 teaspoon rosemary
3 cups water

Cut off woody stems of asparagus; cut into 1-inch pieces. In large soup pot, bring water to boil and dissolve bouillon. Add asparagus, potatoes, onion, lemon juice and spices. Bring to a boil and simmer until vegetables are tender, about 10 minutes. Place half of mixture in blender or food processor; cover and blend until smooth. Pour into a large bowl. Repeat with remaining mixture and set aside. In same soup pot, melt butter or margarine. Stir in flour, salt and pepper to make a thick paste. Add milk all at once. Cook and stir on medium-high heat until mixture is thickened and bubbly. Stir in vegetable mixture. Season to taste with additional salt and pepper.

ANGELA D. NOBLE

Thou shalt not weigh more than thy refrigerator.

TOMATILLO CHICKEN SOUP

Tomatillos are small green tomatoes native to Mexico—you'll find them in the produce department of large grocery stores. They have a papery brown husk that you remove before washing. All ingredients in this soup combine well to make a flavorful light entree.

1 medium onion, chopped
3 to 4 garlic cloves, minced
1 cup brown rice
3 tablespoons olive oil
8 cups tomatillos
2 cups green chilies
12 cups chicken broth
4 cups chicken, cooked and cubed
1/4 cup cilantro, chopped
2 teaspoons ground comino
Salt to taste
2 teaspoons pepper

Garnish:
Sour cream and fresh cilantro sprigs

In a stock pot, sauté onions, garlic and brown rice in the olive oil until onions are soft and the rice is golden. Place tomatillos in boiling salted water for about 3 minutes. Drain and discard cooking water. Place tomatillos and chilies in food processor. Pulse several times to chop coarsely. Add tomatillos and chilies to onion-rice mixture. Add remaining ingredients. Taste for salt and pepper. Cook for about 15 to 20 minutes until rice is done. Garnish with a dollop of sour cream and a sprig of cilantro. Serves 20.

Cynthia Pedregon
Peach Tree Tea Room
Fredericksburg, Texas

SEVEN BEAN SOUP
(GIVE OR TAKE A FEW)

This soup blend, with recipe instructions, makes a nice holiday gift.

2 cups mixed beans (suggested mixture below)
2 ¹/₂ quarts water
2 slices bacon
1 large onion, coarsely chopped
3 cloves garlic, minced
1 (10 ounce) can Rotel tomatoes with chiles
1 pound country-style breakfast sausage, browned
2 teaspoons lemon juice
Salt to taste

Wash and pick over the beans carefully. Place in a large pot and cover with 2¹/₂ quarts of water. Soak at least 2 hours if possible. Bring to a boil. Remove from flame. Discard water and fill with fresh water and bring to a boil again with the bacon slices. Add the chopped onion and garlic. Bring to a boil again, reduce heat and cook over low heat for 1¹/₂ hours or until all beans are soft but not mushy or falling apart. Add the tomatoes with chiles and cook for 30 minutes. Add the sausage which has been browned and drained. Add the lemon juice and salt to taste. Remove and discard bacon slices. Simmer soup for a few more minutes and then serve hot with corn or tortilla chips. (For variety, serve the last of the soup over rice).

To make the seven-bean blend: Take 1 pound each of the following beans and peas: Lima beans, kidney beans, pinto beans, navy beans, lentils, black beans and split green peas. Mix well in a large bowl or put in a large glass jar and shake.

A little hug goes a long way: a big hug goes even further.

ITALIAN VEGETABLE SOUP

1 pound ground beef
1 cup diced onion
1 cup sliced celery
1 cup sliced carrots
2 cloves garlic, minced
1 (16 ounce) can tomatoes
1 (15 ounce) can tomato sauce
1 (15 ounce) can red kidney beans, undrained
2 cups water
5 teaspoons beef bouillon granules
1 tablespoon dried parsley flakes
1 teaspoon salt
$1/2$ teaspoon oregano
$1/2$ teaspoon sweet basil
$1/4$ teaspoon black pepper
2 cups shredded cabbage
1 cup frozen or fresh green beans, cut in 1-inch
    pieces (optional)
$1/2$ cup small elbow macaroni
Parmesan cheese

Brown beef in large heavy kettle; drain. Add all the ingredients except cabbage, green beans and macaroni. Bring to boil. Lower heat; cover and simmer 20 minutes. Add cabbage, green beans and macaroni; bring to boil and simmer until vegetables are tender. If you prefer a thinner soup, add additional water or broth. Sprinkle with the Parmesan cheese before serving.

POSOLE

I usually make this a day ahead to allow the flavor to "ripen". This also freezes well. This is another of my husband Gordon's most requested recipes.

2 quarts water (1 ¹/₂ quarts if no meat is used)
4 teaspoons vegetable broth concentrate
I pound pork, cut in cubes (optional)
I can hominy (I prefer white hominy)
3 to 4 potatoes, cubed
I can green chile sauce or Rotel tomatoes and chilies, diced
¹/₂ teaspoon oregano
3 cloves garlic, minced
Salt and pepper to taste

Combine all ingredients in a large soup pot, bring to a boil, reduce heat, and simmer until meat is cooked, or about 45 minutes to 1 hour.

CHILI SOUP

I ¹/₂ pounds ground beef
I large can tomato juice
I large can tomatoes, puréed in blender
I large can chili
I can pinto beans or cooked dried beans or pork and beans
Chili powder, salt and pepper to taste

Sauté the ground beef, add other ingredients and simmer 45 minutes. This is thinner than chili, but still has that chili flavor.

HOT TOMATO JUICE SOUP

³/₄ cup chopped onion
2 stalks celery, chopped
2 tablespoons butter or margarine, melted
2 quarts tomato juice
2 teaspoons low-sodium beef-flavored bouillon granules
2 teaspoons Worcestershire sauce
2 teaspoons Dijon mustard
¹/₄ teaspoon hot sauce
Lemon slices (optional)
Celery leaves (optional)

Sauté onion and celery in butter in a Dutch oven until transparent. Add tomato juice and next 4 ingredients. Bring to a boil; reduce heat, and simmer 10 minutes. Garnish with lemon slices and celery leaves, if desired. Yield: 10 cups.

U. S. SENATE BEAN SOUP

1 pound bag Great Northern beans (or navy beans)
1 large onion, chopped
2 ribs celery, chopped
1 clove garlic, minced
1 bay leaf
1 can tomatoes, puréed
Salt and pepper to taste
Sausage (optional)

Wash beans. Cover with 3 quarts water and bring to a boil. Cover and turn off heat for 1 hour. Return to heat and bring to a boil again. Add rest of ingredients and simmer 2¹/₂ to 3 hours until beans are soft Purée beans in blender, a little at a time, adding liquid to make a fairly thick soup. May be served with slices of browned sausage.

 53

MOM'S CHICKEN SOUP

*Mom's little secret is that the yellow food coloring makes
the soup a rich golden color which is very appetizing.*

I chicken (about 2 ¹/₂ to 3 pounds.) with giblets, quartered
2 ¹/₂ quarts water
I tablespoon salt
I medium onion
6 whole peppercorns
6 celery stalks, divided (leaves reserved)
6 whole carrots, divided
2 cups cooked rice or cooked fine egg noodles
¹/₄ cup chopped fresh parsley
3 to 4 drops yellow food coloring

Put chicken, giblets, water, salt, onion, peppercorns, 3 stalks celery, all the celery leaves and 3 carrots in a soup kettle. Cover and bring to a boil. Skim off the foam. Reduce heat to simmer and cook 2 hours or until meat is tender. Remove meat, vegetables, peppercorns and giblets. Discard cooked vegetables, peppercorns and giblets. Strain stock, if desired.

Chill stock, then skim fat layer. Dice remaining celery and carrots; add to stock. Cook until vegetables are tender. Meanwhile, remove chicken from bones and dice. Add chicken, cooked rice or noodles and parsley. Heat through. Stir in food coloring. Yield: 10 to 12 servings.

SPLIT PEA SOUP

1 pound package split peas
1 large onion, minced
1 rib celery and leaves, minced
1 large clove garlic, minced
1 teaspoon cayenne
1 teaspoon thyme
$^1/_2$ teaspoon sage
1 $^1/_2$ teaspoons salt
1 bay leaf
1 $^1/_2$ cups chicken stock
1 cup minced salt pork or bacon

Soak peas overnight in 2 quarts water. Fry salt pork or bacon and remove. In fat from fried meat, sauté vegetables until brown. Add rest of ingredients to peas, cover and cook slowly for 2$^1/_2$ hours.

VERY VEGGIE THREE CAN SOUP

I "made up" this recipe one cold, rainy day. It tastes just like fresh vegetable soup and is low fat and good for you. It keeps well in the refrigerator and is better the second day.

2 cans Freshcut diced tomatoes
1 can Veg-all
2 potatoes, diced
1 onion, chopped fine
1 tablespoon vegetable bouillon
1 teaspoon salt
$^1/_2$ teaspoon pepper
3 cans water

Bring all ingredients to a boil in a large soup pot. Cover, turn heat down, and simmer one hour.

GREEN CHILE STEW

This is often requested on cold winter days by my husband,
Gordon. Make it a day ahead of time to let flavors blend, but
you may have to hide it to keep it from being eaten!

1 pound ground beef
1 pound ground pork or 2 pounds pork cubes
1 #3 can tomatoes
1 clove garlic, minced
1 teaspoon garlic powder
Salt, pepper, oregano, coriander to taste
8 to 10 green chiles, chopped, or 1 can green chiles
Diced potatoes
Water to cover

Brown beef and pork. Add remaining ingredients and simmer for
45 minutes.

★

RANCH STEW

My children grew up on this tasty dish and still ask for it. The
recipe can be doubled so you will have some to freeze. Like
most soups and stews, it's better the second day.

1 pound ground beef
1 medium onion, chopped
1 green pepper, chopped
1 (12 ounce) can corn
1 (15 ¹/₂ ounce) can kidney beans
1 (16 ounce) can tomatoes
2 teaspoons chili powder
³/₄ teaspoon salt, pepper to taste

Sauté beef, onion and green pepper until brown. Drain. Add corn, beans and tomatoes and simmer until slightly thickened and reduced (approximately 45 minutes). Serves 6.

CARMEN'S BEEF STEW

My friend, Carmen Dickerson, gave me this recipe years ago. It is a good recipe to put in the oven when you are going to be away from home all day and want a nice meal waiting at day's end. If you prefer a brown stew, substitute 2 cups water and 2 beef bouillon cubes for the tomatoes, tomato sauce and water.

2 pounds cubed beef
2 carrots, in chunks
I cup celery, sliced
1 1/2 cups sliced onion
I can tomatoes
I can water
I (8 ounce) can tomato sauce
I clove garlic, minced
2 tablespoons sugar
Potatoes, cut in chunks

Combine all ingredients and cook in covered casserole for 5 hours at 250 degrees. Add potatoes last 1 1/2 hours.

BLACK-EYED PEA SOUP WITH SALSA AND SOUR CREAM

My daughter, Angela, is a wonderful and inventive cook.
This hearty soup is pretty spicy, and seriously low fat!

I pound dried black-eyed peas, washed and picked over
I ¹/₂ to 2 quarts well-flavored vegetable stock or water
2 bay leaves
¹/₂ teaspoon dried oregano
¹/₂ teaspoon dried basil
I tablespoon cumin seeds
I teaspoon dried summer savory
I teaspoon cracked coriander seeds
Black pepper to taste
2 tablespoons tomato paste
I cup additional vegetable stock or water
I cup spicy hot V-8 vegetable juice
I tablespoon Pickapeppa or Worcestershire sauce
I teaspoon tamari/shoyu soy sauce
I teaspoon Tabasco or similar hot pepper sauce
2 salt-free Morga vegetarian bouillon cubes (Knorr brand
    works great)
3 cloves garlic, peeled and put through a garlic press
I to 2 tablespoons mild vegetable oil
I large onion, chopped
2 medium carrots, scrubbed or peeled, and finely diced
I large green pepper, stemmed, seeded and diced
2 ribs celery with leaves, finely diced
Salt and pepper to taste
Garlic oil (optional)
Salsa for garnish
Sour cream or plain yogurt, for garnish
Fresh cilantro sprigs, for garnish

Spray a large heavy pot with non-stick cooking spray, and in it soak the peas in the stock or water to cover overnight. The next day, add enough of the remaining stock or water to cover the peas by 2 inches. Bring to a boil, then turn down the heat to very low, and add the bay leaves, oregano, basil, cumin seeds, savory, coriander seeds, and several generous grinds of black pepper. Cover the beans and let them simmer, stirring occasionally, until thoroughly soft and cooked. Keep the soup over low heat.

Dissolve the tomato paste in the additional cup of stock or water, and add it to the simmering black-eyes with the V-8, Pickapeppa or Worcestershire sauce, soy sauce, Tabasco sauce, Morga cubes and garlic. Give the mixture a good stir to combine.

Spray a 10-inch skillet with non-stick cooking spray, and in it heat the oil over medium heat. Add the onion and sauté until transparent, about 4 minutes. Add the carrots, green pepper and celery and continue sautéing until they soften a bit, another 2 minutes. Stir these vegetables into the simmering soup, scraping the skillet to get out any little flavorful bits. At this point the soup will be on the thick and stew-like side; if you want it soupier, add additional stock. Add salt and pepper and garlic oil (if desired); simmer uncovered another 15 minutes. Ladle the hot soup into bowls, and top each serving with salsa, a dab of sour cream or yogurt, and a sprig of cilantro. Pass additional salsa, sour cream or yogurt at table.

Angela D. Noble

MARINATED BLACK-EYED PEA SALAD

*Jack includes this anecdote with his recipe: My great-aunt and uncle had a
vegetable farm in Manor, Texas during the 1940's and 1950's. Grandma
would gather the older grandkids to harvest the last of the black-eyed peas.
After picking, we would gather under a big shade tree and shell peas into
a large washtub for hours, all for the reward of a popsicle.*

3 (15 ounce) cans of black-eyed peas, drained
1 large jar pimento, drained
1 bell pepper, diced
4 green onions with tops, diced
1 package Good Seasons Italian dressing mix
Cider vinegar
Cooking oil
¹/₈ teaspoon garlic powder
¹/₄ teaspoon seasoned salt
¹/₈ teaspoon pepper

Mix the salad dressing according to package directions, using the
called for amount of vinegar and oil. Add 2 extra tablespoons of
vinegar. Combine all ingredients and refrigerate overnight, stirring
occasionally. Makes 2 quarts. Serve over lettuce leaves as a cold salad,
or with raw vegetable spears for a light lunch.

JACK CLAGETT

THREE, FOUR OR FIVE BEAN SALAD

This is Karen's mother's recipe and a traditional 4th of July dish in her family. She says she has experimented with changing the bean combinations, and they all work!

$^3/_4$ **cup sugar**
$^1/_2$ **cup cider vinegar**
$^1/_2$ **cup oil - canola or olive**
2 cans green beans
2 cans pinto beans
$^1/_2$ **cup chopped green pepper**
2 cans waxed beans
2 cans black-eyed peas (optional)
2 cans black beans (optional)

Combine sugar, vinegar and oil. Drain beans. Toss in large bowl with oil mixture. Chill in refrigerator at least 24 hours.

KAREN HOWELL

 ★

ENGLISH PEA SALAD

Goes well with fried or barbecued chicken, and is a staple at potlucks!

1 large can LeSoeur peas
2 teaspoons minced onion or $^1/_2$ teaspoon onion powder
Small jar chopped pimientos, drained
Salt, pepper, paprika
$^1/_4$ **pound diced cheese**
1 stalk celery, chopped
$^1/_2$ **cup mayonnaise or salad dressing**

Mix all ingredients and moisten with mayonnaise. Serves 4.

DON'S WOP SALAD MIX

*This recipe from Louisiana has been around for ages but bears
repeating. This is excellent mixed with salad greens.*

1 cup celery, chopped
¹/₂ cup bell pepper, chopped
¹/₂ cup onion, chopped
1 dill pickle, minced
1 dozen ripe olives, chopped
10 cloves garlic, pressed
1 teaspoon capers
1 ¹/₂ cups olive or cooking oil

Mix all ingredients, except oil. Add oil and mix well. Let set in refrigerator for 4 days before using on green salad. Makes 1 quart.
Keeps well in refrigerator.

═══════ ★ ═══════

BLUE DOG BLACK BEAN SALAD

*This recipe takes time, as it needs to marinate, but is well
worth the effort. It can also be used as a dip.*

¹/₃ cup corn oil
¹/₄ cup fresh lime juice
3 tablespoons cilantro, chopped
1 tablespoon pickled jalapeno, minced
1 teaspoon garlic, minced
¹/₂ teaspoon salt
¹/₂ teaspoon ground cumin
1 (16 ounce) can black beans, rinsed and drained
    (Progresso are best)
¹/₂ cup red onions, chopped
¹/₂ cup red peppers
¹/₂ cup yellow peppers

In a large bowl, stir oil, lime juice, cilantro, jalapeno, garlic, cumin and salt. Add beans (make sure you drain and rinse them). Add onions and peppers; stir until all ingredients are well coated. Cover, refrigerate several hours or overnight. Serves 6.

Blue Dog Inn
New Braunfels, Texas

GREEN SALAD WITH PECANS AND APRICOTS

This recipe came from Laurie Locke in Georgetown, Texas. Laurie has a gourmet restaurant, caters, and shares her recipes via the local newspaper.

6 ounces dried apricots, cut into strips
¹/₃ cup dry sherry
³/₄ cup toasted pecan halves
¹/₂ cup extra virgin olive oil
¹/₄ cup balsamic vinegar
Garlic salt and black pepper to taste
6 to 8 cups bite-sized Romaine lettuce

To toast nuts, place in single layer on baking sheet and place in a 350 degrees oven until lightly toasted. Watch carefully. Cool. Place apricot slices in a glass measuring cup or small microwave-safe bowl. Add sherry and cover with plastic wrap. Microwave on high for 3 minutes. Remove and allow to sit for 2 minutes. Cool uncovered for at least 5 minutes. Combine oil, vinegar, garlic salt and pepper. Mix well. Add apricots and pecans to dressing. Toss greens with dressing to coat.

Pat Frase

★

A pat on the back has a ripple effect, like a pebble thrown into water.

PEAR AND FETA SALAD WITH PECANS

While vacationing in California, we were served this salad. When we returned, I experimented until I duplicated the taste and presentation. This is a very elegant salad for a dinner party.

I bunch romaine lettuce or any mixed salad greens
4 ripe pears, peeled and sliced
I cup feta cheese, crumbled

Arrange greens on individual salad plates; divide pear slices among the plates, arranging in a circular pattern; sprinkle Feta cheese over the greens and pears. Dribble 1½ tablespoons dressing over the salads and top with the sugared pecans.

SUGARED PECANS

¹/₄ cup sugar
I egg white
2 cups pecans
Dash of salt

Beat sugar, egg white and salt with a fork until frothy. Add pecans and mix to coat pecans with the mixture. Pour pecans onto a foil-lined cookie sheet in a single layer and bake at 325 degrees for 20 minutes until crisp. Cool.

PERFECT DRESSING

2 cups salad oil
³/₄ cup raspberry vinegar
I teaspoon sugar
I teaspoon salt
¹/₄ teaspoon onion powder

Blend all ingredients in food processor until completely emulsified. This dressing is good on all types of salad, but especially on salads that need a tart sweetness.

ELLY'S COLE SLAW

*This recipe was always taken to or served at barbecues in the
neighborhood, at family gatherings and at church suppers.*

1 head cabbage
¹/₄ cup pimiento
³/₄ cup salad olives
1 cup Hellmann's mayonnaise
¹/₂ cup sour cream
1 ¹/₂ teaspoons garlic salt
¹/₃ teaspoon pepper

Shred or chop cabbage. Drain pimiento and add to cabbage. Drain
salad olives; add to cabbage. Combine mayonnaise, sour cream,
garlic salt and pepper. Mix well with cabbage. Chill well. An extra
delicious ingredient is one pound of cooked, deveined boiled shrimp
tossed in with the ingredients. Serves 8 to 10.

JANIE MACREDIE
GUADALUPE PIT SMOKED MEAT CO.
GRUENE TEXAS

MUSTARD COLE SLAW

*My mother always made cole slaw this way. It is different from
most other cole slaws. It makes a nice meatless meal when served
with red beans and rice, and cornbread, of course!*

I small head cabbage, finely shredded
³/₄ cup mayonnaise or salad dressing
I teaspoon yellow mustard
I teaspoon celery salt or celery seed
I teaspoon salt if using celery seed
¹/₂ teaspoon black pepper

Combine mayonnaise, mustard and spices. Fold into shredded cabbage and mix well. Refrigerate 2 to 3 hours to allow flavors to ripen.

OLD-FASHIONED COLE SLAW

I medium head cabbage, shredded
I carrot, finely grated
I green pepper, chopped
I small onion, sliced
⁷/₈ cup sugar

DRESSING

I cup vinegar
2 tablespoons sugar
³/₄ cup vegetable oil
I tablespoon salt
I tablespoon powdered mustard
I tablespoon celery seed

Combine cabbage, carrot, green pepper and onion. Pour ⁷/₈ cup sugar over all, but do not stir. In saucepan, combine dressing ingredients and bring to rolling boil. Pour immediately over cabbage and mix.

Cover and refrigerate 4 to 6 hours. Mix and serve. Better after 2 to 3 days. Keeps in refrigerator up to 3 weeks. Serves 8.

ELENORA KOHLENBERG

PAMPELL'S EGG SALAD

Pampell's Drugstore in Kerrville is a trip down memory lane. This simple egg salad is very traditional.

4 hard-boiled eggs, chopped coarsely
¹/₂ stalk celery, finely chopped
¹/₄ cup mayonnaise
Salt and pepper to taste

Stir all ingredients together. Ready to serve on fresh bread.

SANDY AND JON WOLFMUELLER
PAMPELL'S DRUGSTORE
KERRVILLE, TEXAS

MACARONI FIESTA SALAD

This is very good with brisket or barbecued chicken.

3 cups cooked elbow macaroni
8 ounces sharp cheddar cheese, cubed
³/₄ cup salad dressing (low-fat okay)
I cup chopped celery
¹/₄ cup chopped pimiento
2 tablespoons chopped green pepper
I tablespoon grated onion or I teaspoon onion powder
Salt and pepper to taste

Combine all ingredients, toss lightly and season to taste. Sprinkle with paprika.

TOMATO-RICE SALAD

When you have a little rice left over, turn it into a tasty salad with this recipe.

1 cup cooked chilled rice
2 medium diced tomatoes
1 tablespoon parsley
$1/4$ cup sliced green onions (or 1 teaspoon onion powder)
2 tablespoons sliced green olives
$1/3$ cup chopped celery

Mix with dressing and chill. Serve on lettuce leaves.

DRESSING

2 tablespoons salad oil
1 tablespoon wine vinegar
$1/4$ teaspoon dry mustard
$1/8$ teaspoon paprika
Dash garlic powder
Dash cayenne
$1/4$ teaspoon salt

Combine all ingredients in a bottle and shake well.

A perfect example of minority rule is a baby in the house.

TACO SALAD

*Is there anyone who doesn't love a good taco salad? This recipe
has been around for years. Store leftovers covered in the refrigerator.
It's good the next day, even if the lettuce wilts.*

1 ½ pounds lean ground beef
1 cup chopped green pepper
1 ½ cups chopped onion
Salt and pepper to taste
1 tablespoon chili powder
6 to 8 dashes cumin
1 (1 pound) box Velveeta
1 small can Rotel tomatoes with green chilies
1 head iceberg lettuce, torn in pieces
2 medium tomatoes, chopped
1 (6 ounce) bag corn chips

Brown meat well in large skillet. Drain. Add chopped pepper and
onion. Season to taste with salt and pepper. Brown a few minutes
more. Add chili powder and cumin. Meanwhile, melt cheese over
very low heat (or in microwave) and stir in tomatoes with green
chiles. In large bowl, arrange in this order: Lettuce, torn in bite-sized
pieces; chopped tomatoes; crumbled corn chips; hot meat mixture;
and hot cheese mixture. Toss and serve immediately. Serves 4 to 6.

A good friend warms the heart.

CYNTHIA'S CHICKEN SALAD

*This is best if made several hours ahead or
the day before to allow flavors to blend.*

4 cups cooked, cubed chicken breasts
8 celery ribs, chopped
6 green onions, thinly sliced
¹/₄ finely chopped yellow onion
¹/₄ cup capers, undrained
¹/₂ cup Peach Tree Herb Mayo
¹/₂ cup Hellmann's prepared mayonnaise (not salad dressing!)

Place all ingredients in mixing bowl. Toss lightly until combined.
Refrigerate until ready to serve.

PEACH TREE HERB MAYO

¹/₂ cup fresh parsley sprigs
1 green onion
¹/₄ teaspoon minced garlic
3 eggs
1 tablespoon lemon juice
1 ¹/₂ teaspoons apple cider vinegar
1 ¹/₂ teaspoons whole grain Pommery or Dijon mustard
Dash of Tabasco
1 teaspoon salt
¹/₂ teaspoon white pepper
1 ¹/₂ teaspoons dill weed
2 ¹/₄ cups oil

Combine all ingredients except oil in a food processor or blender.
Process until chopped fine and well blended. With machine running, slowly add oil, allowing the mayonnaise to thicken as the oil
is added. Makes 4 cups.

CYNTHIA PEDREGON
PEACH TREE TEA ROOM
FREDERICKSBURG, TEXAS

BROCCOLI SALAD

1 bunch broccoli
1 small onion, chopped
1 cup sunflower seed nuts
1 cup raisins
12 slices bacon, cooked and crumbled
1 cup mayonnaise
$^1/_2$ cup sugar
2 tablespoons vinegar

Wash broccoli and drain. Cut off florets and cut in bite-sized pieces. (Save the heavy stems to use in soup.) Combine the florets with the onion, sunflower seed nuts, raisins and bacon. In a small bowl, combine the mayonnaise, sugar and vinegar until well blended. Pour over the broccoli mixture and stir lightly. Cover bowl and refrigerate until ready to serve. Serves 6.

MARILYN ZENGLER

BRISKET SALAD

Use leftovers from Never Fail Brisket to make this delicious main-course salad. Serve with French bread.

1 to 2 cups leftover brisket, chopped small
    (from Never Fail Brisket recipe)
4 cups romaine lettuce, torn in bite-sized pieces
1 tomato, chopped
$^1/_3$ to $^1/_2$ cup feta cheese, crumbled
$^1/_3$ cup La Martinique True French Vinaigrette Dressing

Toss all salad ingredients with the dressing. This brand of dressing is available in supermarkets. It is not low-fat, but is worth it for the taste. This is a delicious main dish salad.

HEISSER KARTOFFELSALAT

Hot Potato Salad

6 medium potatoes
¹/₄ cup onion, finely chopped
6 strips bacon, diced
¹/₂ cup cider vinegar
1 ¹/₂ tablespoons sugar
1 teaspoon salt
Coarsely ground black pepper

Cook potatoes in boiling salt water until tender. Peel and cube. Season with salt and pepper. Fry bacon until crisp; add to potatoes. Heat onion in bacon fat until partly done, then add vinegar and sugar to onion and bacon fat; heat to boiling point. Pour over potatoes and mix lightly. Serve at once. Serves 6. This salad keeps well when refrigerated and is good served cold.

JULIA A. FISCHER
FISCHER & WIESER'S SPECIALTY FOODS
FREDERICKSBURG, TEXAS

FIVE CUP SALAD

No holiday dinner is complete without this
pretty and delicious fruit salad. It's a tradition!

1 cup pineapple chunks
1 cup mandarin orange slices
1 cup very finely grated coconut
1 cup small marshmallows
1 cup sour cream

Drain oranges and pineapple. Mix all ingredients, cover and chill overnight. Stir several times and return to refrigerator until ready to serve. Serves 8.

THANKSGIVING WALDORF SALAD

2 bananas, peeled and sliced
2 fresh pears, cored and diced
¹/₃ cup celery, sliced
¹/₄ cup walnut pieces
2 tablespoons salad dressing
2 tablespoons sour cream
1 tablespoon lemon juice
1 teaspoon sugar or honey
¹/₈ teaspoon ground ginger

Place bananas, pears, celery and walnuts in salad bowl. Combine remaining ingredients in small bowl; mix well. Pour over fruit, tossing lightly to coat. Serve in lettuce-lined salad bowls, if desired.

THE TIMMERMANN SISTERS
GERONIMO, TEXAS

COCA COLA SALAD

This old-fashioned salad was always present at potlucks, church suppers and holiday gatherings. It's not only pretty; it's good, too.

1 package Dark Cherry Jello
1 cup chopped pecans
1 (6 ounce) CocaCola
1 can dark Bing cherries, drained (save 1 cup juice)
1 can chunk pineapple, drained (save juice)

Heat 1 cup cherry juice and add to Jello, stirring until dissolved. Add enough pineapple juice to CocaCola to make 1 cup. Pour into Jello mixture, stir. Refrigerate Jello mixture until partially congealed and add drained cherries and pineapple. Return to refrigerator until completely congealed. Cut in squares and serve on lettuce leaves.

BOB AND MARILYN KEYS

MARY'S FRUIT SALAD

1 large can chunk pineapple
2 small cans mandarin oranges
4 bananas, sliced
1 large package instant vanilla pudding
$^1/_2$ cup pecans, chopped
$^1/_2$ cup maraschino cherries, halved

Drain pineapple and oranges, reserving liquid. Measure 2 cups reserved juice and mix with the vanilla pudding mix. Add fruit and nuts, stirring to blend. Top with maraschino cherry halves.

HONEY MUSTARD DRESSING

This dressing is best if it is served after allowing it to sit for 24 hours under refrigeration. This recipe makes a large quantity, but may be halved.

2 quarts mayonnaise
1 $^1/_4$ cups honey
$^1/_4$ teaspoon cayenne pepper
1 teaspoon onion salt
1 $^1/_4$ cups French's mustard
1 $^1/_4$ cups vegetable oil
$^1/_2$ cup apple cider vinegar

Warm the honey in a microwave or under hot running water. Mix all of the ingredients well (including the honey) with a wire whisk.

SALTGRASS STEAK HOUSE
HOUSTON, DALLAS AND
SAN ANTONIO, TEXAS

CREAMED BEANS, CABBAGE OR TURNIPS

*This is a favorite vegetable recipe of the Gruene family,
and works well with any of these vegetables*

Green Beans:
fresh, cut French style, flour and water, or

Cabbage:
shredded, bacon, flour and water, or

Turnips:
purple top turnips, flour and water
Butter

Beans: Cut French style, sprinkle with small amount of flour. Melt butter in pan. Add floured beans and stir over heat. Don't brown! Add water, cover and cook until tender; season with salt and pepper.

Cabbage: Shred and cook until done, covering with as little water as possible. Cut several slices of bacon in squares, fry until crisp, add some flour and mix well. Add liquid from cabbage; stir and add cabbage; season with salt and pepper.

Turnips: Cut in thin slices and quarter. Boil, just covering with water. When done, thicken with flour and water; season with salt, pepper and a pat of butter.

KYLE AND ETHELENE GRUENE
GRUENE, TEXAS

Organized people are just too lazy to look for things.

SAVORY BLACK BEANS

Black beans need proper seasoning or they will be very bland. Try this recipe. These are good over rice or with any Southwestern meal.

¹/₂ pound black beans, washed and picked over
I quart water
¹/₄ cup olive oil
¹/₂ large onion, minced
2 cloves garlic, minced
I ham bone
¹/₂ teaspoon salt
¹/₂ teaspoon oregano
2 bay leaves
I teaspoon cumin

In a large pot, place the beans and water. Soak overnight or at least 3 or 4 hours. In a medium skillet, heat the oil until hot. Sauté the vegetables until translucent. Add the vegetables, seasonings and ham bone to the beans and bring to a boil. Turn the heat down low and simmer until very tender, stirring occasionally. Add more water if necessary. The beans should be very tender and almost soupy when they are done. The ham bone can be omitted for a good vegetarian dish.

DON'T TRY TO TEACH A PIG TO SING. IT WASTES YOUR TIME AND ANNOYS THE PIG

RED BEANS OR PINTO BEANS

Red (or pinto) beans and rice were a staple at our table when I was growing up. My Cajun grandmother always cooked her beans this way.

I pound red or pinto beans
I large onion, chopped
I clove garlic
I teaspoon thyme
I teaspoon salt
¹/₂ teaspoon cayenne

Wash beans in several changes of water and pick over. Cover with water and soak overnight or several hours. When ready to cook, add remainder of ingredients and bring to a boil over high heat. Turn heat down to simmer, cover, and cook about 2 or 3 hours until soft. Add water if needed. When beans are very soft, if they seem too soupy, bring the pot to a boil again and boil down, watching carefully, until the juice is thick and creamy. Turn off heat and mash a few beans to further thicken the juice. Serve over rice for a one-dish meal.

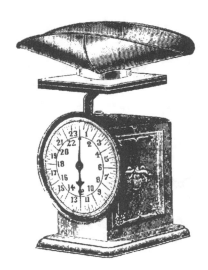

MARILYN'S BAKED BEANS

These are "Arkansas" baked beans, and traditional at cookouts and potlucks.

4 slices bacon, cooked and crumbled
2 tablespoons bacon drippings
$1/2$ cup green onion tops, chopped
$1/2$ cup green pepper, chopped
2 (1 pound) cans pork and beans
2 tablespoons brown sugar
2 tablespoons Worcestershire sauce
Black pepper
1 teaspoon prepared mustard

Cook 4 slices bacon, reserving 2 tablespoons of drippings. Sauté onion and green pepper in bacon drippings, until pepper is no longer crisp. Add bacon, onion and green pepper to pork and beans, stirring in brown sugar, Worcestershire sauce, pepper and mustard. Place in baking dish and bake uncovered $1^1/2$ hours at 325 degrees.

BOB AND MARILYN KEYS

RANCH ROUND UP

1 to 2 jars D. L. Jardine's Texacante Salsa and Dip
$1/2$ bunch broccoli, separated into small florets
$1/2$ head cauliflower, separated into small florets
1 red onion, sliced
1 green pepper, sliced
4 carrots, sliced
1 jar D. L. Jardine's Texas Caviar
2 cups cooked rice

Basically you just "round up" all your favorite garden fresh vegetables, put them in a large sauté pan, cover with D. L. Jardine's

Texacante Salsa, and simmer on low for about 30 minutes. Once cooked, generously pour your "Round Up" mixture over rice and Yee Haw you've got one great meal! Feel free to add grated cheese or sour cream.

NATALIE HARDAGE
JARDINE'S FOODS OF TEXAS

GERMAN RED CABBAGE

2 tablespoons bacon drippings
4 cups shredded red cabbage
2 cups cubed unpared apple
¹/₄ cup brown sugar
¹/₄ cup vinegar
¹/₂ teaspoon caraway seed
1 ¹/₄ teaspoons salt
Dash of pepper

Heat drippings in skillet; add remaining ingredients and ¹/₄ cup water. Cook covered over low heat; stir occasionally. For crisp cabbage cook 15 minutes; for tender, 25 to 30 minutes.

RONNIE SCHRIEWER

GREAT CARROTS

1 pound carrots, sliced thin
¹/₂ stick butter, melted
¹/₂ cup lemon juice

Melt butter and lemon juice together. Toss with carrots and bake at 375 degrees for one hour.

OKRA AND TOMATOES

*This southern version of okra "gumbo" takes advantage of the
abundant fresh okra available during central Texas summers.*

1 pound fresh okra
$^1/_2$ large white onion, coarsely chopped
$^1/_2$ large bell pepper, coarsely chopped
2 ribs of celery, sliced into $^1/_4$-inch pieces
2 tablespoons olive oil or cooking oil
2 (15 ounce) cans of tomato pieces, with juice
$^1/_4$ teaspoon salt
$^1/_8$ teaspoon pepper

Select the smallest okra pods so seeds will be small. Trim the tops
and tips and cut into $^1/_2$-inch pieces. Wash and set aside in colander.
In a large skillet, sauté the onion, bell pepper and celery in the oil at
medium heat for about 10 minutes. Add the tomatoes and liquid,
salt and pepper and simmer uncovered for another 10 minutes. Add
the okra and simmer with cover on for about 15 minutes or until the
okra is tender but retains its shape. Serves 6 to 8 as a side vegetable,
or over white rice as an entree.

JACK CLAGETT

OKRA, TOMATOES AND CORN DRESSING

My family recipe from Louisiana is practically a complete meal.
Served with black-eyed peas, sliced tomatoes and
cornbread, it is a reminder of my small town childhood.

1 pound okra
1 onion, chopped
1 clove garlic, minced
1 medium can tomatoes
1 can corn, or frozen or fresh corn cut off the cob
¹/₂ cup uncooked rice
¹/₄ cup olive oil
¹/₂ cup water
1 teaspoon salt
¹/₄ teaspoon pepper

Cut okra into slices; brown with onion and garlic in hot oil in a heavy skillet. When vegetables are brown, add rice and brown 2 - 3 minutes. Add tomatoes with juice, drained corn, and water. Bring to a boil, cover tightly and turn heat down to simmer. Cook about 15 to 20 minutes until water is absorbed and rice is done. Season to taste with salt and pepper.

ROMANO POTATOES

*This wonderful potato dish is very popular
in the Saltgrass Steakhouse restaurants.*

5 pounds new potatoes
¹/₄ pound cooked and chopped bacon
¹/₂ bunch green onions
¹/₄ pound melted butter
I cup shredded Monterey Jack cheese
I ¹/₂ cups shredded cheddar cheese
I cup heavy whipping cream
I tablespoon Lawry's seasoned salt
¹/₃ tablespoon cracked black pepper
¹/₃ tablespoon white pepper
¹/₂ tablespoon paprika
¹/₄ cup Romano cheese

There are a few preliminary steps that need to be accomplished before beginning this recipe: boil the new potatoes until tender and allow to cool. Next, cook the bacon and set aside. Once the potatoes have cooled, quarter them. Chop the bacon into small pieces and dice the green onions, using only the green part. Now that these preliminary steps have been completed, carefully mix the new potatoes, chopped bacon, green onions, Monterey Jack cheese and cheddar cheese. In a separate container, mix the heavy whipping cream, melted butter, Lawry's Seasoned Salt, cracked black pepper, white pepper and paprika. Add this liquid mixture to the potato mixture and mix well. Once these ingredients have been well mixed, place into a greased baking pan. Sprinkle the top with the Romano cheese. Bake uncovered in the oven at 350 degrees for approximately 15 minutes or until heated throughout. Serve hot!

SALTGRASS STEAKHOUSE
HOUSTON, DALLAS AND
SAN ANTONIO, TEXAS

MUNA'S SCALLOPED POTATOES

*At family gatherings, scalloped potatoes were always
served with baked ham. This was my mother's recipe.*

8 cups potatoes, peeled and sliced 1/4-inch thick
4 cups milk
3 tablespoons cornstarch
2 teaspoons salt
1/2 teaspoon pepper

Mix cornstarch with 1 cup milk in a small bowl, stirring until smooth.
Add this mixture to the remainder of the milk, add salt and pepper,
and mix thoroughly. In a large, deep greased casserole mix the potatoes with the milk mixture. Dot with butter and bake at 375 degrees
for 45 minutes to 1 hour. The casserole may be covered during the
first 25 to 30 minutes, but should be uncovered to brown.

CHEESY POTATO BAKE

4 large unpeeled baking potatoes
1/4 cup butter or margarine
1 tablespoon grated onion
1 teaspoon salt
1/8 teaspoon pepper
1 teaspoon dry barbecue seasoning
1 cup shredded cheddar cheese
1 tablespoon chopped fresh parsley

Slice potatoes and stagger in greased shallow 2-quart baking dish.
In small saucepan, heat butter, onion, salt, pepper and barbecue seasoning. Drizzle over potatoes. Cover and bake at 375 degrees for 45
minutes or until tender. Sprinkle with cheese and parsley. Bake uncovered until cheese melts.

ELENORA KOHLENBERG

GERMAN POTATOES

*My grandmother used to say this was a good dish to serve
when there was "month left at the end of the money."*

5 to 6 red potatoes, unpeeled, sliced ¹/₄-inch thick
1 onion, sliced
¹/₄ cup oil
Salt and pepper

In a large heavy skillet, melt ¹/₄ cup oil or bacon drippings. Add potatoes and onion, stirring occasionally, and cook for 5 to 10 minutes until the vegetables begin to brown nicely. Add ¹/₂ cup water, cover tightly, and turn heat to low. Stir occasionally to prevent sticking (more water may be needed) until vegetables are tender and water is absorbed. Season with salt and pepper and serve.

CRUSTY POTATO PANCAKES

6 medium potatoes, peeled
1 small onion, grated
3 eggs
³/₄ cup flour
2 teaspoons salt
Oil for frying

Grate potatoes coarsely into a bowl filled with cold water. This keeps the potatoes from turning dark and removes some of the excess starch, making the pancakes crispier. In another bowl, combine the onion, egg, flour and salt. Drain potatoes, pressing out all liquid. Beat potatoes into batter. Heat oil. Spoon heaping tablespoons of batter into oil, spreading batter with the back of the spoon into 4-inch rounds. Brown on one side, turn and brown on the other side. Brown the pancakes slowly, so potatoes will have a chance to cook through properly. Drain on absorbent paper. Serve hot with applesauce.

Cynthia Hartmann Nealeigh

ONION ROASTED POTATOES

2 pounds potatoes, scrubbed and cut into chunks
¹/₃ cup olive oil
1 envelope onion soup mix
1 tablespoon rosemary

Preheat oven to 450 degrees. Put all ingredients in a large plastic bag and shake until potatoes are thoroughly coated. Place potatoes in a shallow baking pan. Bake 40 minutes, stirring occasionally, until potatoes are brown and tender. Serves 8.

CANDIED SWEET POTATOES

1 large can sweet potatoes, drained
¹/₂ cup butter, melted
2 eggs, separated
Juice of 1 orange
2 tablespoons sugar
2 tablespoons milk
1 teaspoon vanilla

Topping:
5 tablespoons butter
1 cup packed brown sugar
1 cup pecan halves, dusted with 1 tablespoon flour

Preheat oven to 350 degrees. Spray casserole with cooking spray. Mash potatoes, stir in butter, egg yolks, orange juice, sugar, milk and vanilla. Beat egg whites until soft peaks form. Fold into sweet potatoes. Spoon into casserole. Make the topping by melting the butter, stirring in the sugar and pecans. Spread topping on potato mixture. Bake for 25 minutes. This can be prepared ahead and kept in the refrigerator until ready to bake.

RUMPLETEE-THUMP

*My mother-in-law, Daphne Hughes, who was a World
War II war bride from England, gave me this recipe.*

Mashed potatoes, freshly made or left over (about 3 cups)
Small head of cabbage, shredded and cooked until tender
Grated cheese, about 1 cup
Chives
Chopped leftover ham or browned seasoned
    ground beef (optional)

Preheat oven to 350 degrees. Mix mashed potatoes, cooked cabbage, and chives to taste. Place in a greased casserole. If using meat, layer meat between two layers of potato-cabbage mixture. Top with grated cheese. Bake 30 minutes.

SPINACH SOUFFLE

This is a nice luncheon dish or side dish for dinner.

¼ cup margarine
¼ cup flour
¾ cup milk
½ teaspoon salt
¼ teaspoon pepper
1 cup shredded sharp cheese
(10 ounce) package frozen chopped spinach, thawed and
squeezed dry
1 tablespoon chopped onion
4 eggs, separated

Slightly beat egg yolks. In separate bowl, beat egg whites until stiff peaks form. Make a cream sauce with margarine, flour, milk and seasonings. Add cheese, stirring until melted. Remove from heat;

stir in spinach and onion. Gradually add in beaten egg yolks; cool. Fold the spinach mixture into stiffly beaten egg whites; pour into a greased 1 1/2-quart dish at least 6 inches tall. Bake at 350 degrees for 35 minutes. Serve immediately.

SPINACH MADELEINE

I have made this recipe for years and it never fails to have admirers. This is definitely better if made the day before you plan to serve it. It also freezes well. Freeze before baking.

2 packages frozen chopped spinach

4 tablespoons butter

2 tablespoons flour

2 tablespoons chopped onion

1/2 cup evaporated milk (low-fat works fine)

1/2 cup vegetable liquor

1/2 teaspoon black pepper

3/4 teaspoon celery salt

3/4 teaspoon garlic salt

1/2 teaspoon salt

6 ounce roll Jalapeno cheese

1 teaspoon Worcestershire sauce

Red pepper to taste

Cook spinach according to directions on package. Drain, reserving vegetable liquor. Melt butter in sauce pan, add flour and onion and cook on low heat until onion is soft. Add milk and vegetable liquor slowly, stirring constantly. Cook until smooth and thick; add seasonings and cheese which has been cut into small pieces. Stir until cheese is melted. Combine with cooked spinach. Pour into greased casserole and bake at 350 degrees for 30 minutes, until hot and bubbly.

ELABORATE SPINACH

This only looks elaborate - it is easy to prepare and a pretty dish.

2 packages frozen spinach
3 large or 6 small tomatoes
¹/₂ teaspoon garlic powder, divided
¹/₄ cup breadcrumbs
1 teaspoon dried, minced onions
4 tablespoons melted butter
¹/₄ teaspoon salt
¹/₃ cup Parmesan
¹/₂ teaspoon thyme
2 beaten eggs

Cook and drain spinach; peel and slice tomatoes into thick slices and lay in bottom of greased flat baking dish. Sprinkle with ¹/₄ teaspoon garlic powder. Mix spinach with breadcrumbs, onion, butter, salt, Parmesan, ¹/₄ teaspoon garlic powder, thyme and eggs. Spoon on top of tomato slices and bake at 350 degrees for 15 to 20 minutes.

SWEET RICE

Use this as a side dish instead of potatoes.
Feed to your grandchildren—they love it!

1 cup uncooked rice
1 tablespoon butter
1 teaspoon salt
1 teaspoon nutmeg
2 cups water
³/₄ cup sugar
Whole milk

Cook rice with butter, salt and nutmeg in water, slowly with lid on, until rice is tender. Add milk until rice is covered (if too thick after coming to a boil, add a little more milk). Stir gently often; add sugar. Simmer until milk is absorbed, but do not let rice dry out too much. Pour into shallow bowl and sprinkle with cinnamon and sugar.

ELEANOR COLDEWAY

SOUR CREAM RICE

3 (4 ounce) cans Ortega chopped green chilies
3 cups sour cream
1 large can pitted black olives, sliced
6 cups cooked rice
¹/₂ pound Monterey Jack cheese, cubed
1 cup cheddar cheese, grated
Paprika
Salt and pepper to taste

Add chilies to sour cream; add ¹/₂ can sliced olives and cubes of Monterey Jack cheese; add to hot rice. Bake at 350 degrees for 30 to 45 minutes. Sprinkle with grated cheddar cheese and decorate with remainder of olives and paprika.

BROWNED RICE

*This simple recipe is delicious and can be made ahead
and reheated. It can be doubled or tripled for a crowd.*

1 medium onion, chopped fine
1/2 stick margarine
1 cup uncooked rice
1 can beef consomme
1 (8 ounce) package fresh mushrooms, sliced
1 cup water

Sauté onion in margarine in heavy skillet. Add rice, consomme,
mushrooms and water. Bake in 9 x 13-inch uncovered casserole in
350 degree oven, stirring occasionally, for 25 to 30 minutes.

BROCCOLI-RICE CASSEROLE

*This can be put into 2 casseroles - one to eat, one to freeze. It is best
made a day ahead. Our family always has this at holiday meals.*

3 packages frozen chopped broccoli
1/2 stick butter or margarine
1 cup celery chopped
1 onion, chopped fine
1 bunch green onions, chopped, including green part
1 pound mushrooms, sliced
2 cups uncooked rice
2 cans cream of mushroom soup
2 cans cream of chicken soup
1 pound Mexican Velveeta

Cook rice until done. Meanwhile, finely chop the vegetables and
sauté until soft in butter. Add chopped broccoli and soups and mix
well. When rice is done, add cheese cut in cubes and mix until melted.
Mix vegetable/soup mixture into rice. Bake at 350 degrees for 1 hour.

TEXAS PECAN PILAF

My friend, Margaret, brought this pilaf to our dinner group
and everyone liked it. The pecans add a nice crunch.

2 tablespoons olive oil
¹/₂ cup each, diced: red and yellow bell peppers and red onion
3 celery ribs, diced
1 medium carrot, diced into ¹/₄-inch pieces
¹/₂ cup wild rice
2 cups regular long-grain rice
4 cups defatted chicken stock
¹/₂ cup butter
¹/₂ cup each, chopped: toasted pecans and green onions
Salt and pepper, to taste

Heat oil in a large saucepan. Add peppers, onion, celery, carrot and wild rice; sauté until soft. Stir in long-grain rice, then stir in stock and butter. Bring to a boil, reduce heat to a simmer and cook, covered, until rice is done, about 15 minutes. Fluff with a fork. Stir in pecans and garnish with chopped green onion. Makes 8 to 10 servings.

MARGARET BROWN

If you can't sing good, sing loud.

MAMA'S RICE DRESSING
Dirty Rice

*This was a staple at Sunday dinner at my grandparents'
house when I was a child. Dinner was always at 12 o'clock
noon or Papa wanted to know what we were waiting for!*

2 cups uncooked rice
4 cups water
1 teaspoon salt
2 to 3 chicken livers
1 onion, finely chopped
¹/₂ green pepper, finely chopped
3 stalks celery, finely chopped
3 green onions, chopped (white and green part)
¹/₄ to ¹/₂ cup chicken broth

To cook rice: Combine rice, water and salt in large heavy saucepan;
bring to a boil, turn down to simmer, and cover. Cook 20 minutes.
Let rest with cover on to allow any excess water to become absorbed.
Sauté vegetables in butter; remove. Sauté chicken livers until no pink
remains; mash. Mix mashed livers and vegetables into rice. Add
broth as needed to make the mixture the consistency of dressing.

RATATOUILLE

¹/₂ cup olive oil
2 cloves garlic, crushed
I large onion, sliced into thick rings
4 medium zucchini, sliced
I medium eggplant, peeled and diced
I green pepper, seeded, cut into rings
4 medium tomatoes, quartered (or I can tomatoes, drained)
2 teaspoons salt
¹/₂ teaspoon pepper
¹/₂ cup black olives (optional)

Heat olive oil in skillet; sauté garlic and onion for a few seconds. Add remaining ingredients, except olives. Sauté about 15 minutes until tender, turning occasionally to cook thoroughly. Serve hot, garnished with olives, as a side dish. Served cold, it is an excellent appetizer when offered with crackers. Makes 10 servings.

SQUASH DRESSING

5 or 6 yellow squash, sliced
I onion, chopped fine
I teaspoon salt
¹/₂ teaspoon pepper
I can cream of mushroom soup
¹/₂ package Pepperidge Farm Cornbread Dressing Mix
I cup chicken or vegetable broth (use I chicken or vegetable
    bouillon cube in I cup hot water)

Cook onion and squash in a very small amount of water until tender. Drain, add rest of ingredients and mix well. Pour into greased casserole. Bake at 350 degrees for 30 minutes until brown.

SPAGHETTI SQUASH CASSEROLE

*This is delicious. If you haven't tried spaghetti squash because you
don't know what to do with it, look for it in the supermarket.*

I **spaghetti squash, cooked and shredded with fork
(see instructions below)**
I **cup sour cream**
8 **ounces Monterey Jack cheese, with or without jalapenos,
shredded**
I **onion, chopped (may use green onion, also, if desired)**
I **bell pepper, chopped**
¹/₂ stick butter

To cook spaghetti squash; cut in half, place face down and wrap in
plastic wrap. Microwave on high for 10 to 15 minutes, turning every 4 or 5 minutes. Shred with fork. Sauté onion and bell pepper in
butter. Mix with shredded squash and remaining ingredients; bake
in greased casserole at 350 degrees for 30 to 40 minutes.

CARMEN'S GRITS

I usually double or triple this recipe and freeze the extra to have on hand.

I **cup grits (not instant)**
I **teaspoon salt**
4 **cups water**
I **stick butter**
¹/₄ pound Velveeta
¹/₄ pound sharp cheese, grated or cubed
¹/₃ cup milk (optional)

Cook grits in salted water according to package directions. Add rest
of ingredients and mix, stirring occasionally until cheese and butter
are melted. Pour in 1 ¹/₂ -quart greasedcasserole. Bake 1 hour at 325
degrees. Serves 8. (If freezing, freeze before baking).

CORN CASSEROLE

*Una and I go back a long way. She used to drive a shocking pink '59 Ford,
so I can hardly believe she actually turned out to be a grownup lady
who cooks! She says she makes this for family dinners at holidays.*

2 cans whole kernel corn
1 large jar pimientos
1 large green bell pepper
1 onion
1 box Uncle Ben's long grain and wild rice
2 cups Velveeta cheese
Salt to taste
1 tablespoon black pepper

Chop green pepper and onion. Cook in skillet sprayed with cooking spray, until onion is clear. Cube 2 cups Velveeta cheese. Prepare and cook rice according to directions on box. Drain 2 cans of corn (can reserve small amount of liquid from one can). Combine all ingredients. Stir to melt cheese. Place in a large greased casserole dish. Bake at 375 degrees for 30 minutes.

UNA HUTCHINS

Grandmas are just antique little girls.

FRIED CORN

*Whoever eats the most corn also eats the most corn silk! This
is a delicious way to prepare corn when it is fresh and juicy.*

Fresh corn on the cob (2 ears per person)
¹/₂ stick butter
Salt
Pepper

Cut kernels off the ears of corn and then scrape the cobs with a
knife, stripping off the "milk" from the cobs. Melt the butter in a
saucepan or skillet and add the corn, cooking slowly and stirring
occasionally for 10 minutes or so, until the corn has released the rest
of its liquid and has cooked down a little but is not dry. Season with
salt and pepper and enjoy.

CONFETTI

I onion, grated or chopped very fine
8 tablespoons butter, divided
I chicken or vegetable bouillon cube
2 zucchini, shredded
2 yellow squash, shredded
I pound carrots, shredded
2 stalks celery, chopped fine
I green pepper, chopped fine
¹/₄ teaspoon nutmeg
¹/₄ teaspoon pepper

Sauté onion in 2 tablespoons butter until soft. Crush in the bouillon
cube. Remove from heat. Add the rest of the vegetables and the spices
and mix well. Melt the remaining butter, pour over the top of the
mixture and sauté quickly over medium high heat until vegetables
are just done. Serves 8.

WHAT'S FOR DINNER, MOM?

The front of the **Gruene General Store**, with its screen door, authentic antique advertising signs and "sittin' bench" where one can sit and watch the world go by while enjoying a cool soft drink, 5 cent cup of coffee or hand-dipped ice cream cone, is a delightful reminder of the way life used to be.

Gruene General Store's historical medallion, granted by the Texas Historical Commission, tells the story of how the frugal German, Henry D. Gruene re-used his original frame building by moving it across the street when he decided to construct a new, two-story brick building. In the early 1970's the entire town was declared a National Historic District to protect it from being demolished. The owners of all the buildings in Gruene have banded together to prevent the modernization of the exterior structures and to preserve the integrity of the vernacular architecture of the period.

Today the Gruene General Store's soda fountain, with its colorful old advertising and delicious hand-dipped Blue Bell ice cream, soft drinks, and 5 cent cup of coffee, take you back to the good old days with a reminder of how life used to be.

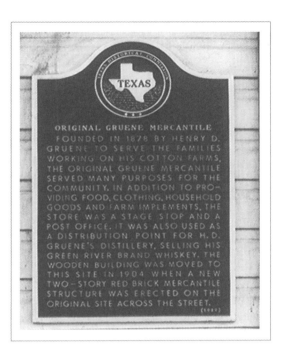

Customers enjoy a "Moon Pie and an RC Cola", along with hand-dipped Blue Bell ice cream, soft drinks, old fashioned lemonade with real lemon slices floating in it, or a 5 cent cup of coffee at the Gruene General Store soda fountain while entertaining themselves by reading the antique advertising signs or listening to the country music played in the store.

EGGS A LA GRUENE MANSION INN

Definitely not low-fat, but this is an elegant and delicious brunch dish.

$^1/_2$ **pound American cheese, cubed**
$^1/_2$ **pound Velveeta cheese, cubed**
1 (8 ounce) carton sour cream
4 ounces cream cheese
1 (10 ounce) can Rotel diced tomatoes and green chiles
4 whole wheat croissants
20 eggs (yes, allow 5 per person in this recipe)
$^1/_2$ **green bell pepper, diced**
Pico de Gallo (optional)

In a microwave-safe dish combine the American and Velveeta cheeses, sour cream, cream cheese and tomatoes. Microwave or cook over a low flame until melted. Set aside but keep very hot.

Slice the croissants through the center as for a sandwich. Place on an ungreased cookie sheet. Bake in a 350 degree oven for 20 minutes.

In a large bowl, beat the eggs until very frothy and scramble in a large buttered skillet over medium heat. When the eggs are almost done, add the diced green pepper. Remove the croissants from the oven and place together on plates or a serving platter so they form a round base for the eggs. Pile scrambled eggs over the croissants. Pour the cheese sauce over all. Make certain the sauce is very hot and thin enough to sink to the bottom of the croissant. Serve with Pico de Gallo, if desired. Makes 4 servings.

SHARON & BILL McCASKILL
GRUENE MANSION INN
GRUENE TEXAS

It's difficult to think anything but pleasant thoughts while eating a home-grown tomato.
—Lewis Grizzard

BREAKFAST DELIGHT CASSEROLE

This recipe is a favorite with the guests of the Gruene Homestead Inn. Make it the night before to make breakfast preparation easier in the morning; serve with fresh fruit and muffins and have salsa on the tables for folks who like it hot!

2 (6 ounce) boxes cheddar cheese croutons
1 (8 ounce) package cheddar cheese, shredded
1 pound bulk sausage, cooked and drained
    (regular or hot and spicy)
1 dozen eggs
Nature's Seasoning Blend
2 cups milk
1 small can drained, or ³/₄ cup fresh, sliced
    mushrooms (optional)
1 small can diced green chilies, drained (optional)

Lightly coat a 9x13-inch glass (Pyrex) casserole dish with butter flavored non-stick cooking spray. Spread croutons evenly on the bottom. Add in the following order: cheese, mushrooms, chilies, sausage. Break eggs into a large bowl and season with Nature's Seasoning Blend to taste. Beat with a whisk. Add milk and beat again. Pour over ingredients in pan. Cover and refrigerate overnight. Bake in a preheated 350 degree oven for 30 to 40 minutes. Do not overcook, as it will get dry. Let sit 5 minutes before cutting and serving. Yield: 8 to 12 servings.

BILLIE MILES
GRUENE HOMESTEAD INN
GRUENE TEXAS

OREGANO EGGS

A nice Southwestern touch to this dish is to offer salsa along with the eggs.

2 cups shredded cheddar cheese
3 tablespoons flour
3 teaspoons dry oregano
4 eggs
2 cups half-and-half
18 small mushrooms
¹/₂ cup chopped green onions

The night before: spray 6 (8 ounce) baking dishes with non-stick cooking spray. Clean and thickly slice 3 small mushrooms into each baking dish. Top each with 2 tablespoons chopped green onions. Cover each dish with plastic wrap and refrigerate. Combine cheddar cheese, flour, oregano, eggs and half-and-half; cover and refrigerate.

One hour before breakfast: Preheat oven to 350 degrees. Pour cheese and egg mixture over mushrooms and onions. Bake 35 minutes (they pop up high when done). Let rest 10 to 15 minutes (they will fall). Turn out of baking dish, place right side up on serving plates.

Olympic Lights Bed & Breakfast
Friday Harbor, WA

BARBARA PORTERFIELD'S SAUSAGE STRATA

*This is my standard brunch dish for company or on holidays.
It is even good leftover and warmed briefly in the microwave.*

2 pounds bulk pork sausage
$1/4$ cup each finely chopped sweet red and green
   pepper (optional)
2 teaspoons yellow prepared mustard
12 slices white bread, crusts removed
1 pound Swiss cheese, shredded
6 large eggs
4 cups milk
1 teaspoon Worcestershire sauce
$1/8$ teaspoon ground black pepper
$1/8$ teaspoon ground nutmeg
$1/8$ teaspoon salt

Day before serving, prepare strata: Grease 13x 9-inch baking pan. In
large skillet, sauté sausage and peppers, if using, until sausage is
well browned. Drain off fat well. Stir mustard into sausage mixture.
Arrange bread in bottom of baking pan. Top with sausage mixture
and cheese. In large bowl, lightly beat eggs. Beat in milk,
Worcestershire sauce, pepper, nutmeg and salt. Pour over layers in
baking pan. Cover tightly and refrigerate overnight. Next day, heat
oven to 350 degrees. Bake strata, uncovered, 40 to 50 minutes or
until center seems set. Serve immediately.

FRESH EGGS

WELSH RABBIT

When my children were small, we would often have this on Sunday night for supper. When they asked why it was called Welsh "Rabbit", I told them a story about how the hunters would come home empty-handed from the day's hunt and their wives would make up a cheese sauce over bread. That was their "rabbit".

¼ cup margarine
¼ cup flour
2 cups milk or 1 cup milk and 1 cup beer
½ teaspoon salt
Dash of pepper
¼ teaspoon cayenne
¼ teaspoon dry mustard
8 ounces Old English cheese, cubed
Toast triangles
Paprika

Make a cream sauce with margarine, flour, milk and seasonings. Add cheese, stir until melted. Do not allow to boil. Serve on toast triangles and sprinkle with paprika.

★

STACY'S QUICHE

Elizabeth's daughter, Stacy, makes this and it is wonderful!

2 cups shredded Swiss cheese
2 tablespoons flour
1 ½ cups half-and-half
4 eggs, beaten
³⁄₄ cup ham or sausage
½ teaspoon salt
Dash of pepper
9-inch unbaked pie shell

Toss the cheese with the flour. Add half-and-half, eggs, ham or sausage, and seasonings. Mix well. Pour into pie shell. Bake at 350 degrees for 55 to 60 minutes, or until set. Makes 4 servings.

ELIZABETH BARRY

HAM AND VEGETABLE QUICHE

This recipe came from Michele's great-grandmother.

$^1/_2$ **cup cauliflower, chopped**
$^1/_4$ **cup carrots, chopped**
$^1/_4$ **cup onion, chopped**
$^1/_4$ **cup green onions, chopped**
$^2/_3$ **cup cooked ham, chopped**
1 cup cheddar cheese, shredded
3 eggs, beaten
1 cup milk
$^1/_2$ **teaspoon salt**
Baked and cooled 10-inch pie shell

Cook cauliflower, carrots, onion and green onions in boiling salted water for 5 minutes. Drain. Layer ham and vegetables in pie shell. Sprinkle with cheese. Combine eggs, milk and salt and beat well. Pour into pie shell over vegetables, ham and cheese. Bake at 375 degrees for 40 to 45 minutes. Let stand for 10 minutes before serving.

MICHELE TAYLOR

If you take it out, put it back.
If you open it, close it.
If you throw it down, pick it up.
If you take it off, hang it up.

ANGELA'S HEAVENLY SPANAKOPITA
Greek Pastry Filled with Spinach and Cheese

1 large onion, finely chopped
5 cloves garlic, minced
1 tablespoon basil
1 tablespoon oregano
2 (10 ounce) boxes frozen chopped spinach
2 (10 ounce) boxes frozen chopped broccoli
1 (16 ounce) box frozen phyllo dough
2 tablespoons olive oil
4 tablespoons flour
Olive oil cooking spray
2 (8 ounce) blocks feta cheese, crumbled
1 cup Ricotta cheese

Thaw phyllo, spinach and broccoli. Heat olive oil in deep-sided skillet. Sauté onion, garlic and herbs until onions are soft. Add spinach and broccoli. Stir and cook 3 minutes on medium-high heat. Add flour. Stir and cook 3 more minutes. Remove from heat, add cheese and mix well, adding salt and pepper to taste. Oil a 13x9-inch metal baking pan. Lay a sheet of phyllo in pan, allowing sheet to overlap sides of pan. Spray sheet with olive oil spray. Repeat until you have 8 sheets layered on top of one another. Spread half of the filling on top, then repeat with another 8 sheets, using the same procedure as before. Spread the remaining filling on top. Layer and oil the rest of the phyllo on top. Tuck corners inside pan and give it a final spray. Bake uncovered at 375 degrees until brown and crispy, about 30 to 40 minutes. Serves 6 to 8.

ANGELA D. NOBLE

CONNIE'S CHICKEN TETRAZZINI

5 pound hen, boiled tender and cubed
7 ounce package spaghetti cooked in chicken stock
1 large can mushrooms (with juice)
1 bell pepper
1 large onion
$^{1}/_{2}$ pound butter
1 cup flour
1 quart milk
$^{1}/_{2}$ pound American cheese
$^{1}/_{2}$ pound Old English cheese
Salt and pepper to taste

Cook mushrooms, bell pepper and onion in mushroom juice until tender (5 to 10 minutes), then set aside. In saucepan, melt butter. Add flour and stir 1 minute. Add milk and cheeses and cook slowly until cheese is melted. Add salt and pepper to taste. Mix together cheese sauce with cubed chicken, cooked spaghetti and cooked mushroom mixture. Cover with buttered breadcrumbs and bake 30 to 40 minutes at 325 degrees. Serve very hot.

CONNIE CONE

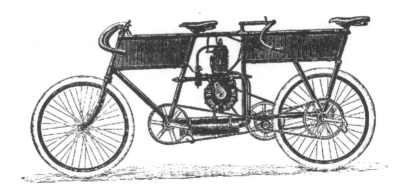

AUSTRIAN CHICKEN STRUDEL

*This is an easy, but elegant way to serve chicken. It always
draws raves when we serve it. Garnish each serving with
a dollop of sour cream and a fresh rosemary sprig!*

4 green onions, finely chopped
¹/₃ pound fresh mushrooms, sliced
2 tablespoons butter
4 cups cooked cubed chicken
¹/₂ teaspoon salt
¹/₄ teaspoon pepper
2 tablespoons chopped parsley
¹/₂ teaspoon tarragon
2 eggs, beaten
1 ¹/₂ cups grated Swiss cheese
16 sheets phyllo pastry
¹/₂ cup butter, melted

Garnish:
sour cream

Sauté onions and mushrooms in 2 tablespoons butter until tender.
In a bowl, combine the onion-mushroom mixture, chicken, salt, pepper, parsley and tarragon. Stir in eggs and cheese. Lay out 1 sheet of
phyllo pastry and brush with melted butter. Place another sheet of
phyllo pastry on top of the first and brush with butter. Spoon ²/₃ cup
of chicken filling along one end of the rectangle, leaving a margin of
2 inches in from the end as well as on both sides. Fold in both ends
and loosely roll up the strudel. Brush with butter and place on a
greased baking sheet. Repeat this process until filling is used up.
Bake in a preheated 400 degree oven for 35 minutes, or until crust is
golden brown. Garnish with a dollop of sour cream. Each strudel
serves 1 person. Makes 8 strudels.

Cynthia Pedregon
Peach Tree Tea Room
Fredericksburg, Texas

CHICKEN ORIENTAL

This is also good with leftover turkey and is a
good way to use up all that Thanksgiving bird.

1 cup sliced onion
1 green pepper, julienne sliced
4 tablespoons butter
1 can mushrooms or 8 ounces fresh mushrooms, sliced
3 cups chicken, cut up
1 cup diced celery
2 1/2 cups chicken broth
4 tablespoons cornstarch
1/8 teaspoon pepper
3 tablespoons soy sauce
1 tomato in wedges
2 cans Chinese noodles

Sauté onions and green pepper in butter 3 minutes. Add drained mushrooms and chicken to skillet. Cook over low heat 10 minutes; add celery. Mix 1/4 cup broth with cornstarch to make a paste. Add remaining broth to skillet; cook until hot. Stir in cornstarch mixture. Cook, stirring constantly, until sauce is bubbling and thickened. Stir in pepper, soy sauce, and tomatoes. Cook slowly 5 minutes. Serve over crispy Chinese noodles.

CHICKEN AND BISCUIT PIE WITH LEEKS

This recipe makes a very large casserole and is definitely worth the effort. The leeks add an interesting touch and the dish is very attractive with the biscuit topping.

CHICKEN AND LEEK FILLING

2 (3 to 3 ¹/₂ pounds) chickens, quartered
2 large onions, peeled and quartered
3 carrots, cut into 2-inch pieces
2 whole cloves of garlic, peeled
2 bay leaves
I bunch fresh thyme, tied with kitchen string
I leek, sliced into 1/8-inch rounds
I tablespoon vegetable oil
Salt and pepper to taste
4 ¹/₂ cups reserved chicken stock
3 tablespoons sweet butter
7 tablespoons flour

Place the chicken, onions, carrots, garlic, bay leaves and thyme in an 8-quart stockpot. Add enough water to cover the ingredients by 2 inches. Bring to a boil, then reduce heat and skim occasionally. Simmer for 30 minutes. Remove chicken from stock and discard vegetables. Reserve 4 ¹/₂ cups of the stock. Soak the leeks in a large bowl of water for one hour to remove the sand. Drain in a colander. Slice, using only white part of leeks.

In a small saucepan over medium-high heat, sauté leeks in the oil until soft. Add ¹/₂ cup of the chicken broth and simmer 5 minutes more. Season with salt and pepper.

Remove the skin from the chicken and cut the meat into 1-inch pieces. Combine chicken and leeks and season with salt and pepper. Spread the chicken and leek mixture evenly in a 12-inch oval baking dish.

In a 9-inch skillet, melt butter over medium-high heat. Whisk in the flour 1 tablespoon at a time. Slowly whisk in the 4 cups chicken stock, stirring until all the stock has been incorporated. Bring to a gentle boil and cook for 2 minutes or until the gravy thickens. Season with salt and pepper. Remove from heat and pour over the chicken-leek mixture.

Preheat the oven to 375 degrees. Place biscuits on top of the chicken-leek mixture and brush with egg wash. Bake uncovered for 30 minutes or until the gravy bubbles and the biscuits are golden brown. Serve with cranberry sauce.

BAKING POWDER BISCUITS

2 cups flour
4 teaspoons baking powder
2 teaspoons salt
Handful of flat-leaf parsley, chopped
¹/₂ cup vegetable shortening or sweet butter
1 ¹/₄ cups milk at room temperature
1 egg beaten with 1 tablespoon milk

In a large bowl, sift together the flour, baking powder and salt. Add parsley. Using a fork or your fingers, incorporate the shortening a few tablespoons at a time until the dough is crumbly. Add 1 cup of milk and blend until a soft dough forms, adding additional ¹/₄ cup of milk as necessary. Turn the dough onto a lightly floured surface and knead dough lightly until it holds together. Add more flour one tablespoon at a time if needed. Don't overwork. Gently roll out the dough to ³/₄-inch thickness. With a 3-inch cookie cutter, cut out the biscuits and let them rest for 5 minutes.

Soul food is just what the name implies. It is soulfully cooked food or richly flavored food, good for your ever-loving soul.
—Sheila Ferguson

CHICKEN SPINACH CASSEROLE

This recipe came from Laurie Locke in Georgetown, Texas.

5 pounds stewing chicken or 2 fryers
5 ounces fine egg noodles
1/4 cup butter
1/2 cup flour
1 cup milk
2 cups sour cream
1/3 cup lemon juice
1 (10 ounce) package frozen spinach, cooked and drained
1 (6 ounce) can mushrooms with juice
1 (8 ounce) can sliced water chestnuts
1 (4 ounce) jar chopped pimientos, drained
1/2 cup chopped onion
2 teaspoons seasoned salt
1/2 teaspoon cayenne
1 teaspoon paprika
1/2 teaspoon salt
2 teaspoons pepper
1 1/2 cups grated Monterey Jack cheese

Cook chicken, reserving broth, and cut into bite-sized pieces. Cook noodles and drain. Melt butter, slowly stir in flour until blended. Add milk and broth. Cook over low heat, stirring constantly until thick. Add all ingredients except chicken, noodles and cheese. Mix well. Fold in noodles. In a large buttered casserole, layer 1/2 of vegetable/noodle mixture, then 1/2 of chicken. Repeat, ending with vegetable/noodle mixture. Top with cheese. Bake at 300 degrees for 25 to 30 minutes, until bubbly. Yield: 6 to 8 servings.

PAT FRASE

OREGANO CHICKEN AND PASTA

This is one of my favorite low-fat, fast and easy recipes.

4 chicken breasts, skinned
1 container low-fat Alfredo sauce, thinned with 2 tablespoons
    water or white wine
¹/₂ teaspoon oregano
1 teaspoon fennel seed, crushed
Salt, pepper and red pepper flakes to taste
2 teaspoons olive oil
2 cloves garlic
2 small or 1 large tomato, chopped
¹/₂ cup Parmesan cheese

Cut breasts in strips ³/₈-inch wide. Season with oregano and fennel. Sauté garlic and tomato in olive oil for 2 to 3 minutes. Add chicken strips and sauté 5 minutes, turning once, until brown and cooked. Cover and cook 5 minutes more until tender. In the meantime, cook 2 cups penne pasta in 6 cups salted water; drain and keep warm. Add Alfredo sauce to chicken strips, season to taste, and simmer 2 to 3 minutes more. Pour over pasta and garnish with Parmesan cheese. Serves 4.

Life's too short to drink cheap beer.

SPAGHETTI SAUCE WITH MEAT

My friend, Carmen, comes from a large and very Italian family.
This is her family recipe, and they know their sauce!

4 (30 ounce) cans Italian pear tomatoes
4 (12 ounce) cans Contadina tomato paste
48 ounces water
¹/₄ cup dried sweet basil (or more, to taste)
³/₄ cup sugar
¹/₈ cup salt
3 cloves fresh garlic, crushed in garlic press
1 bunch fresh parsley (3 to 4 pieces)
3 to 4 leaves fresh sweet basil
Dash pepper
2 to 3 tablespoons Bertolli olive oil
1 large yellow onion, finely chopped
4 stalks celery, finely chopped
3 to 4 ounces Pecorino imported Romano cheese, finely grated
6 pounds lean ground beef
1 teaspoon garlic salt

In blender, combine one 30 ounce can of tomatoes with one 12 ounce can of tomato paste. Blend for 2 to 3 minutes. Pour into a 12 quart pot. Repeat this process three times, using remaining tomatoes and tomato paste. Add 48 ounces of water to pot, using tomato paste cans to measure. Stir in dried sweet basil, sugar, salt and fresh pressed garlic. Add fresh parsley, fresh sweet basil, and pepper.

Heat 2 to 3 tablespoons olive oil in skillet. Add celery and onion, sauté uncovered on low or medium heat until soft; transfer to pot. Sprinkle in Romano cheese. Cook uncovered about 45 minutes on low to medium heat. Watch carefully so that mixture does not scorch on bottom. Brown ground beef in large skillet over medium heat. Season with salt, pepper, sweet basil and garlic salt. (Takes about 30 minutes to brown). In large colander, drain well; add to sauce. Cover and cook on low an additional 2 to 3 hours, stirring every 20 minutes. Watch heat, making sure sauce does not burn on bottom of pan. Periodically taste; add more seasoning, if desired. Remove parsley and basil stems before serving. This makes 6 to 8 quarts sauce. Use glass jars to store or freeze.

CARMEN LUCIA DICKERSON

SPAGHETTI AL PESTO

¹/₃ **cup olive oil**

I cup firmly packed parsley leaves

I teaspoon dried basil leaves or I large sprig fresh basil

I clove garlic

¹/₂ **cup grated Parmesan cheese**

2 tablespoons pine nuts or coarsely chopped walnuts

I tablespoon butter or margarine

¹/₂ **teaspoon salt**

¹/₄ **teaspoon pepper**

¹/₂ **pound spaghetti, cooked**

In an electric blender, combine oil, parsley, basil, garlic, cheese, nuts, butter, salt and pepper. Blend at high speed to a pastelike consistency, about 1 minute. Toss together with the hot spaghetti and serve immediately. Serves 4.

ONE DISH PASTA

This is a very tasty meal that can be made up with what's on hand in the refrigerator and is also good without the meat for a vegetarian meal. A firm, rather large type of pasta is preferable to angel hair pasta in this dish.

4 cups penne pasta
I bunch fresh broccoli
8 ounces ham strips or bacon bits
8 ounce container cream cheese with chives and onions
¹/₃ cup milk

Cook pasta, drain and set aside. Cook broccoli in same pot. Drain and set aside. Again in the same pot, blend cream cheese with milk. Heat thoroughly, add cooked broccoli, pasta and meat and toss gently to blend.

★

PASTA WITH PINE NUTS

8 to 12 ounces angel hair pasta
2 to 4 cloves garlic, minced
¹/₄ cup olive oil and I to 2 tablespoons butter or margarine
2 tablespoons prepared pesto
Butter Buds, generous sprinkling
¹/₄ cup fresh chopped parsley
I tablespoon each chopped fresh basil and oregano
White ground pepper to taste
¹/₄ teaspoon salt or onion salt or powder
2 generous cups of chopped and seeded Roma tomatoes
¹/₂ cup roasted pine nuts
4 to 6 ounces feta cheese
Freshly grated Parmesan cheese

Cook pasta according to package directions. Heat oil in large skillet. Add minced garlic and butter and sauté quickly. Add pesto, several shakes of Butter Buds, the chopped herbs and seasonings. Heat just until hot. Toss in tomatoes, and when heated, pour mixture over the cooked pasta, which has been drained and placed on a platter. Sprinkle on top the pine nuts, crumbled feta cheese and freshly grated Parmesan. Variations: Add chopped artichoke hearts or black olives or calamata olives.

★

PASTA WITH TOMATOES ALFREDO

Refrigerated low-fat Alfredo sauce may be the greatest invention since sliced bread. It can be the basis for many tasty meals.

8 to 12 ounces penne pasta
1 carton low-fat Alfredo sauce
3 cloves garlic, minced
1 tablespoon olive oil
4 to 5 Roma tomatoes, chopped
1 tablespoon basil
Salt and pepper
1 can sliced black olives
Grated Parmesan or Romano cheese

Cook pasta according to package directions. Sauté garlic in oil, add chopped tomatoes and spices. Cook 10 minutes, add olives and Alfredo sauce. Simmer 5 more minutes. Serve over pasta. Top with Parmesan or Romano cheese. Grilled chicken may be added on top of the pasta before pouring the sauce over for a more substantial dish.

HELPFUL HINT:

It's not necessary to peel garlic cloves before crushing in a garlic press.

VEGGIE LASAGNA

The lasagna noodles don't have to be cooked before putting into a casserole to be baked! (Saves a pot.) This recipe is even easier if prepared spaghetti sauce is used. A nice variation is to peel and thinly slice a small eggplant and layer it, instead of the spinach. No, it's not necessary to cook the eggplant first, either!

Sauce:
1 tablespoon olive oil
1 onion, finely chopped
1 clove garlic, finely chopped
4 to 6 Roma tomatoes, chopped
1 bunch fresh basil, chopped
1 tablespoon fennel, crushed
1 teaspoon salt
1 teaspoon sugar
1 container low fat ricotta
1 tablespoon parsley
1 ½ cups Mozzarella, shredded
1 bunch fresh spinach, wilted in microwave and drained
6 lasagna noodles, uncooked

Sauce: Sauté onion in olive oil until soft; add garlic and sauté 1 minute. Add tomatoes and other ingredients and simmer 20 minutes.

Spray pan with non-stick cooking spray; spread ½ cup sauce on bottom of pan. Layer uncooked noodles, spinach, ricotta with parsley stirred in, sauce; repeat and top with Mozzarella. Bake covered at 325 degrees for 30 minutes, then uncovered for 15 to 20 minutes. Can rest a while before serving. Serves 4.

TOMATO PIE

1 precooked pie shell (10 minutes at 400 degrees)
2 to 3 large tomatoes
¹/₂ cup mild white onions
1 cup or more, grated cheddar and/or Monterey Jack cheese
1 cup mayonnaise (low fat okay)
¹/₄ cup green chilies
6 strips cooked bacon, crumbled

Sprinkle about ¹/₄ of cheese in bottom of cooked pie shell. Thick-slice tomatoes (drain tomatoes on paper towel to reduce juice) and fill crust almost to top. Sprinkle bacon over tomatoes. Mix mayonnaise, onions, cheese and chilies and spread over top of pie. Bake 35 minutes at 350 degrees. Serve immediately.

MARGARET BROWN

GERMAN SAUERKRAUT AND SAUSAGE

Serve with cornbread for a one-dish meal.

1 quart sauerkraut (preferably fresh or bottled, not canned)
3 cups water
1 clove garlic
¹/₄ teaspoon dill weed
¹/₄ teaspoon cayenne
1 to 2 pounds sausage (link)
1 large potato, grated

Rinse sauerkraut in cold water; drain. Heat sauerkraut, water, garlic, dill and pepper to boiling. Simmer 30 minutes. Meanwhile, brown sausage (cut in ¹/₂-inch slices). Stir potato into sauerkraut. Add sausage and drippings and simmer until potato has disintegrated and juice is thick and creamy (about 20 to 30 minutes). Stir frequently and add water, if necessary, to keep from scorching or sticking.

BRISKET HASH

This is another good old-fashioned soul-and-tummy satisfying meal. When I was a child, my mother would make this from the remnants of Sunday's pot roast.

2 cups chopped leftover brisket (from Never Fail Brisket recipe)
¹/₂ onion, chopped
2 tablespoons flour
3 tablespoons butter
2 cups beef bouillon (or beef gravy from brisket)
2 or 3 potatoes, cooked and chopped small

Melt butter, brown flour and onions in butter. Add the bouillon and stir and cook on low heat until slightly thickened to make a thin gravy. Add the beef and potatoes and cook until warmed through. Correct seasoning by adding salt and pepper if needed. Serve over toast which has been cut into triangles.

CHUCKWAGON SUPPER

5 strips bacon
5 eggs, beaten
3 or 4 potatoes, cut into small cubes
2 slices Velveeta, cut in strips
1 onion, finely chopped

Fry bacon in skillet, set aside. In bacon grease, fry potatoes and onions. When potatoes are almost done, turn heat to low and pour in the eggs. Crumble in the bacon on top and then top with the cheese strips. Put lid on skillet and cook on very low heat until eggs are firm. Do not stir after the lid is placed on the skillet. Cut in pie shape wedges to serve.

GEFUELLTE NUDELN
Filled Noodles

Noodles:
2 eggs
2 tablespoons water
1/2 teaspoon baking powder
1 cup flour

Filling:
³/₄ pound ground meat
1 small onion, chopped
Salt and pepper

Sauce:
2 cups water
1 tablespoon butter
¹/₂ teaspoon salt
Chili powder (optional)
2 cups canned tomatoes

Noodles: Combine all ingredients thoroughly. Roll out to ¹/₄-inch thickness and cut into 4x4-inch squares. Makes 12 to 14 squares.

Filling: Brown ground meat and onion; season to taste with salt and pepper. Place on noodle squares, fold, and pinch edges together. Drop into sauce.

Sauce: In large pot, combine water, salt, butter, chili powder and tomatoes. Boil 15 to 20 minutes with filled noodles.

Place filled noodles on a platter and serve with sauce.

JULIA A. FISCHER
FISCHER & WIESER SPECIALTY FOODS
FREDERICKSBURG, TEXAS

ALPHABET SOUP MEATBALLS

My children's grandmother gave me this recipe when they were small and they always loved this dish. I'll bet your children or grandchildren will love it, too!

1 pound ground beef
1 cup breadcrumbs
1 egg
1 teaspoon salt
$^1/_4$ teaspoon pepper
$^1/_4$ cup onion, finely chopped
1 can vegetarian vegetable soup
1 soup can evaporated milk
1 package egg noodles, cooked as directed on package

Mix the ground beef, breadcrumbs, egg and seasonings and form 1-inch meatballs. Brown the meatballs in a skillet and pour off the grease. Add the can of soup and evaporated milk and simmer, covered, until the meatballs are done. Serve over the noodles.

STUFFED PEPPERS

4 large bell peppers
$^3/_4$ pound ground beef
$^1/_2$ cup onion, finely chopped
$^1/_2$ cup raw rice
1 cup water or tomato juice
1 teaspoon salt
$^1/_2$ teaspoon pepper

Cut the tops off the bell peppers. In a skillet, sauté the ground beef with the onion until no longer pink. Add the rice and seasonings and stir in the water or tomato juice. Cover and simmer about 15 minutes until the liquid is absorbed and the rice is tender. Allow to cool slightly. Meanwhile, put about 1 inch of water in the bottom of a casserole dish large enough for the four peppers to stand upright. Spoon the meat and rice mixture into the peppers, mounding slightly on top. Breadcrumbs or cheese may be added as a topping during the last 15 minutes of baking. Bake the peppers in a 325 degree oven for 30 to 45 minutes until the peppers are tender.

GOURMET HAMBURGER

This is an out-of-the-ordinary casserole recipe, good enough for company. I've had this recipe for years and it is always good.

1 (8 ounce) package noodles
2 pounds ground round
$^1/_3$ cup chopped onion
1 tablespoon chopped green pepper
2 (8 ounce) cans tomato sauce
1 (8 ounce) package cream cheese, softened
1 cup cottage cheese
$^1/_2$ cup low fat sour cream
$^1/_3$ cup chopped onion

Cook noodles, drain. Brown meat with green pepper and chopped onion. Stir in tomato sauce and season with salt and pepper. Combine cheeses, sour cream and chopped onion. Layer noodles, meat and cheese mixtures. Bake at 350 degrees for 30 minutes. Serves 6.

TEXAS-ITALIAN HOMINY

This is a different ground beef casserole and is very tasty.

1 ¹/₂ pounds ground beef
1 tablespoon chopped onion
1 (6 ounce) stick pepperoni, sliced
¹/₂ cup milk
2 slices cheese, cubed
2 teaspoons cornstarch
1 can tomato sauce
¹/₄ teaspoon garlic juice or ¹/₄ teaspoon garlic powder
1 teaspoon basil
¹/₂ teaspoon oregano
1 tablespoon Parmesan cheese
2 cans hominy, drained
¹/₂ cup grated cheese

Cook ground beef, onion and pepperoni in skillet until brown. Drain off excess fat. Pour milk into saucepan and add cheese. Cook over low heat until melted. Mix ¹/₂ cup cold water with cornstarch and stir into milk. Cook until thickened. Add tomato sauce, seasonings and Parmesan cheese and mix. In one large or two small greased casseroles, layer in the following order: hominy; meat mixture, cheese sauce; and grated cheese. Bake at 350 degrees 15 minutes or until heated through.

The most precious things
in life aren't things.

SHRIMP AU GRATIN

1 (4 ounce) can mushrooms
3 tablespoons chopped onion
3 tablespoons butter, melted
$1/4$ cup flour
$1/2$ teaspoon salt
$1/4$ teaspoon dry mustard
Dash red or black pepper
1 $1/2$ cups milk
1 cup grated cheese
1 pound cooked shrimp, peeled and deveined
$1/4$ cup dry breadcrumbs
$1/4$ cup white wine (optional)

Cook mushrooms and onion in butter until tender. Blend in flour and seasonings. Add milk (and wine, if desired) gradually and cook until thick, stirring constantly. Add $3/4$ cup cheese and stir until melted. Stir in shrimp and pour into well greased casserole. Combine crumbs and remaining cheese, sprinkle over top. Dot with butter. Bake at 400 degrees for 20 minutes. Serves 4.

SHEPHERD'S PIE

*My mother-in-law, Daphne Hughes, is originally from England.
This is her recipe which all the family loves.*

1 ½ pounds **LEAN** ground beef
1 chopped onion
1 cup water
1 teaspoon **Nature's Seasoning**
1 tablespoon **Bisto***
Mashed potatoes

Crumble meat in heavy skillet - turn heat to low. Season with
Nature's Seasoning. Cook until all red is gone from meat. Add water and Bisto. Simmer for 1 to 1½ hours. Turn into casserole. Top
with mashed potatoes. Bake at 375 degrees for 45 minutes.

*Bisto is a beef-flavored starch similar to cornstarch. It is now widely available in
supermarkets. It makes a flavorful gravy.

**Rounding the corner at Gruene Road and Hunter Road, a 1931 Model A
Ford seems right at home in this current photograph of the intersection.
The Gruene Mansion Inn is in the background.**

BLACK EYES OF TEXAS CASSEROLE

This wonderfully tasty casserole is a good dish to serve a crowd. Kids love it.

2 pounds ground beef
1 large onion, chopped
1 (15 ounce) can jalapeno black-eyed peas
1 (10³/₄ ounce) can cream of chicken soup
1 (10³/₄ ounce) can cream of mushroom soup
1 (10 ounce) can hot enchilada sauce
1 teaspoon garlic powder or 2 to 3 garlic cloves, minced
1 (10¹/₂ ounce) bag tortilla chips, divided
3 cups grated cheddar cheese, divided

In a large skillet over medium heat, brown ground beef. Add onion, black-eyed peas, undiluted soups, enchilada sauce and garlic; stir. Grease two casseroles; layer ¹/₄ of chips on bottom of each casserole, then top with ¹/₄ of meat mixture and ¹/₄ of cheese. Repeat layering procedure. Bake in preheated 350 degree oven for 35 minutes. Makes 12 to 16 servings.

Appreciation is like an insurance policy—
it has to be renewed every now and then.

COLD WEATHER CASSEROLE

This is great for the meat-and-potatoes lover.

Filling:
1 (10 ounce) can or package frozen mixed vegetables
3 ¹/₂ cups mashed potatoes
1 pound ground beef, browned and drained
1 teaspoon salt
¹/₄ teaspoon Tabasco sauce

Brown Sauce:
2 tablespoons butter
2 tablespoons flour
1 can beef broth
¹/₄ teaspoon Tabasco

Prepare brown sauce by browning flour in melted butter, stirring constantly. Stir in broth and Tabasco. Simmer, stirring constantly, until sauce thickens and comes to a boil. Add browned, drained ground beef, salt, vegetables and Tabasco to brown sauce. Mix well. Ring a 2-quart casserole with mashed potatoes. Spoon beef mixture into center. Bake 30 minutes at 350 degrees.

PAT TEPE

CHICKEN ENCHILADAS

3 boneless chicken breasts
1 large can cream of chicken soup
1 large container sour cream
1 cup chopped green onions
1 cup grated cheddar cheese
1 cup grated Monterey Jack cheese
1 large red bell pepper
1 tomato, chopped
1 teaspoon curry powder
1 package flour tortillas

Grill or boil chicken breasts and cube. In large bowl combine cubed chicken breast, chopped green onions, cheddar cheese, Monterey Jack cheese, chopped bell pepper and tomato and set aside. Bring to a boil chicken soup and sour cream (milk may be added as needed). Reduce heat and simmer while assembling enchiladas. Spoon small amount of chicken mixture into each tortilla and roll. Place rolled tortillas in large baking dish. Pour sour cream sauce over tortillas. Sprinkle with curry powder. Bake at 350 degrees for 20 minutes or until warm.

ANNA BODE
JEFFERSON GENERAL STORE
JEFFERSON, TEXAS

HELPFUL HINT:

If you get chili pepper in your
eyes or on your skin,
rinse the affected area with milk.

GREEN ENCHILADAS

Easy, fast and good!

1 ¹/₂ pounds ground beef or 2 cups chopped chicken, cooked
1 can chopped green chilies
¹/₂ pound cheese, grated
1 small onion, chopped
1 can cream of chicken soup
1 package tortillas, torn into pieces

Brown ground beef. Combine chilies, cheese, onion and soup; add to meat. Spray casserole with non-stick cooking spray; alternate layers of meat mixture and tortillas in casserole. Bake at 350 degrees for 30 to 40 minutes. Serves 6.

TACO CASSEROLE

This is a quick and easy recipe, and Beth's kids love it!

2 (4 ounce) cans tomato sauce
1 pound ground beef
1 can corn or mixed vegetables, drained
¹/₄ cup finely chopped onion
¹/₂ teaspoon chili powder
1 envelope taco seasoning
1 cup shredded cheddar cheese
Crushed tortilla chips or Nacho Cheese Doritos

Brown ground meat with onion; drain. Add tomato sauce, taco seasoning and chili powder. In greased 13x9-inch glass pan, cover the bottom with crushed chips. Add a layer of the meat mixture. Layer the vegetables and then ¹/₂ cup cheese. Repeat the layering process of the chips and meat mixture, topping with a layer of cheese. Bake in 350 degree oven for 20 to 30 minutes or until cheese is melted.

BETH CROCKER

MUNA'S HOT TAMALE PIE

*My mother, Evelyn Mistrot Keys, used to make this when
I was a child and it is still one of my favorite recipes.*

Crust:
$1/2$ **cup cornmeal**
2 $1/2$ cups water
I teaspoon salt

Filling:
I pound ground beef
$1/2$ **onion, chopped fine**
2 cloves garlic, minced
I tablespoon chile powder
I teaspoon cumin
I tablespoon cornstarch
$1/2$ **cup water**
Shredded cheese to garnish

Crust: Mix cornmeal, water and salt in a medium saucepan. Cook over medium heat, stirring constantly to prevent lumps, until slightly thickened and a thin cornmeal mush is formed. Set aside to cool slightly. It will thicken on standing.

Filling: Brown meat, onion and garlic in a skillet. Add spices and cornstarch, stir to mix and then add water, stirring until thickened. Cook 5 to 10 minutes until meat is tender. While meat is cooking, spread the cornmeal mush in a greased pie pan or casserole, pressing the mush up the sides of the pan to form a crust. Pour the meat mixture into the prepared crust. Bake at 325 degrees for 30 minutes. Garnish with the shredded cheese.

My goal is to weigh what my driver's license says I do.

MEXICAN LASAGNA

This is a very pretty casserole with the green, red, yellow and black strips across the top - nice for a party.

1 ¹/₂ pounds ground beef
1 ¹/₂ teaspoons ground cumin
1 tablespoon chili powder
¹/₄ teaspoon garlic powder
¹/₄ teaspoon red pepper
1 teaspoon salt
1 teaspoon black pepper
1 (16 ounce) can tomatoes, chopped
10 to 12 corn tortillas, torn into quarters
2 cups small curd cottage cheese, drained
1 cup grated Monterey Jack cheese with peppers
1 egg, beaten
¹/₂ cup grated cheddar cheese
2 cups shredded lettuce
¹/₂ cup chopped tomatoes
3 green onions, chopped
¹/₄ cup sliced black olives

Brown ground beef; drain thoroughly. Add cumin, chili powder, garlic powder, red pepper, salt, pepper and tomatoes; heat through.

Spray 13x9x2-inch baking dish with cooking spray; cover bottom and sides of dish with tortillas. Pour beef mixture over tortillas; place a layer of tortillas over meat mixture and set aside. Combine cottage cheese, Monterey Jack cheese and egg; pour over tortillas. Bake at 350 degrees for 30 minutes. Remove from oven; sprinkle rows of cheddar cheese, lettuce, tomatoes, green onions and olives diagonally across center of casserole. Yield: 6 to 8 servings.

SOUTHWESTERN STIR FRY

I found this recipe in a magazine several years ago and my
family has really enjoyed it. It's different, easy, and very good.

8 flour or corn tortillas
I cup salsa
2 teaspoons cornstarch
I tablespoon oil
I medium green pepper, cut in strips
I (12 ounce) can corn, drained
I pound ground beef
3 green onions, sliced
Tomatoes and cheese to garnish

Wrap tortillas in foil and heat in 350 degree oven 10 minutes. Stir salsa and cornstarch together and set aside. Fry pepper, corn and green onion in wok or skillet in oil. Remove. Stir fry ground beef, drain fat, and push to side. Add salsa mixture to wok and cook until thickened. Return veggies to wok, combine with beef and salsa and cook until hot. Serve with tortillas. Garnish with tomatoes and cheese. Serves 4.

SPANISH RICE

This is a quick and easy dinner, and a family favorite.

1 cup uncooked rice
4 tablespoons butter
1 tablespoon green chili peppers, chopped
1 onion, chopped
1 small clove garlic, chopped
1 teaspoon salt
1 tablespoon chili powder
1 cup tomatoes, chopped (canned tomatoes can be used)
1 pound ground meat
1 ½ cups water

Heat ½ of the butter in frying pan; add rice and fry to a light brown, stirring occasionally. Remove rice. Add remaining butter, then fry the meat, onion, garlic and chili peppers about 10 minutes. Add salt, tomatoes and chili powder dissolved in ¼ cup water. Allow mixture to cook a few minutes, then mix with rice. Pour into baking dish, add water and bake at 350 degrees for 45 minutes.

Pat Tepe

CHINESE FRIED RICE

This is a great way to use up leftover meat.

**2 cups diced cooked meat (leftover pork, chicken, ham or
    shrimp)**
2 tablespoons soy sauce
¼ cup oil
I cup uncooked rice
2 ½ cups chicken stock
½ cup sliced onion
¼ cup sliced celery
¼ cup green pepper, sliced
2 eggs, beaten
I cup bean sprouts or Chinese vegetables

Combine meat and soy sauce; let stand. Heat oil, add rice and fry
until golden, stirring. Add meat, stock and onions and simmer until
the rice is tender. Add other vegetables shortly before rice is done.
Cook until liquid is absorbed. Add eggs after pushing rice to one
side of skillet; cook until set, then mix with rice. Serves 6.

WILD RICE AND SAUSAGE

When a good company casserole is needed, try this one. It can be made ahead and refrigerated until time to bake, and it serves a lot of people!

1 pound bulk pork sausage
1 cup chopped celery
1 large onion, chopped
1 medium green pepper, chopped
1 clove garlic, minced
3 cups chicken broth
1 (10 ³/₄ ounce) can cream of mushroom soup, undiluted
1 (10 ³/₄ ounce) can cream of chicken soup, undiluted
1 (8 ounce) can sliced water chestnuts, drained
1 (4 ounce) can sliced mushrooms, drained
1 (6 ounce) package long-grain and wild rice mix
Dash of dried whole thyme
1 (2 ounce) package sliced almonds
Parsley sprigs (optional)

Combine sausage, celery, onion, green pepper and garlic in large skillet; cook over medium heat until sausage is browned and vegetables are tender, stirring to crumble meat. Drain. Stir in remaining ingredients except almonds and parsley; mix well. Spoon into a lightly greased 3 quart casserole, and sprinkle with almonds. Bake at 350 degrees for 1¹/₂ hours. Garnish with parsley, if desired. Yield: 12 servings.

Of all the things I've lost,
I miss my mind the most.

BEEF STROGANOFF

¹/₂ **cup butter**
3 tablespoons oil
1 pound mushrooms, sliced
3 tablespoons chopped green onions
2 pounds lean boneless beef, sliced or cubed
1 cup beef broth
¹/₂ **cup dry vermouth or white wine**
1 teaspoon Worcestershire sauce
¹/₂ **teaspoon tarragon**
¹/₂ **teaspoon rosemary**
¹/₂ **teaspoon parsley**
2 cups sour cream
Salt and pepper to taste

Melt 3 tablespoons butter. Add half the oil. Sauté sliced mushrooms briefly. Add green onions and salt and pepper. Cook 1 minute; reserve. In remaining oil and butter, sauté sliced meat a few pieces at a time until brown. Remove. Add beef broth and vermouth to pan. Cook until volume is reduced by one-half. Add Worcestershire and herbs. Stir in sour cream, beef and vegetables and cook over low heat. Be careful not to boil or sauce will curdle. Serve over rice or noodles. May be made ahead completely and warmed before serving. Serves 6 to 8.

MAMA'S SHORT RIBS

3 to 4 pounds first cut short ribs
¹/₂ cup flour
¹/₄ teaspoon each salt & pepper
2 medium onions, sliced
³/₄ cup catsup
2 tablespoons vinegar
2 tablespoons Worcestershire
4 tablespoons soy sauce
¹/₂ cup sugar
³/₄ cup water

Dust short ribs in flour, salt and pepper and lightly brown on all sides. Slice onions and spread over ribs in baking pan. Combine catsup, vinegar, Worcestershire, soy sauce, sugar and water. Pour over ribs. Bake 3 hours at 300 degrees. Baste often. This sauce is also good on spare ribs! If using spare ribs, bake 2 hours at 300 degrees, then broil last 12 to 15 minutes.

SHARI SHANNON
HUNTER JUNCTION
GRUENE TEXAS

SPIKED ROAST

Eye round roast, pork tenderloin, or beef rump roast
Bacon
Chili petines
Salt and pepper

Cut bacon lengthwise into narrow strips. Salt and pepper both sides of roast. Use a long, slim knife to puncture holes lengthwise through roast. Make as many holes as possible. Take finger and stuff bacon strips into holes. Every other hole, put a chili petine —alternating one at the beginning of hole, next one in the middle of the hole and the next one at the end of the hole. Roast at 350 degrees, 40 minutes per pound. You do not want a rare roast. After the meat is done, remove roast and add water to pan for gravy.

Note: Chile petines are available dried in supermarkets.

KYLE AND ETHELENE GRUENE
GRUENE TEXAS

★

POT ROAST

3 to 4 pound chuck roast
1 tablespoon onion powder
1 teaspoon garlic powder
1 teaspoon salt
¹/₂ teaspoon pepper
4 or 5 potatoes, quartered
6 or 8 carrots, cut in chunks

Season meat on all sides with onion powder, garlic powder, salt and pepper. Brown well in heavy skillet which has been sprayed with cooking spray. Add 1 cup water, turn heat down to simmer, cover skillet tightly and cook slowly for 1¹/₂ to 2 hours. Thirty minutes before the meat is done, add potatoes and carrots. Add more water if necessary to keep meat from sticking, but no more than one more cup. The vegetables will thicken the gravy.

★

Hospitality is one form of worship.
—The Talmud

BEEF BOURGUIGNON

12 slices bacon
6 pounds sirloin cut in 1-inch pieces
2 pounds fresh mushrooms, sliced
4 bay leaves
4 tablespoons parsley
2 teaspoons salt
2 teaspoons thyme
1/4 teaspoon pepper
1 cup flour
1 cup margarine
4 cans consomme
1 can red wine

Cut bacon into small pieces and sauté. Remove bacon and sauté meat in bacon drippings until brown. Discard drippings and reserve beef and bacon. Make a roux by melting 1 cup margarine and browning 1 cup flour, stirring constantly over medium-low heat until very brown, 5 to 10 minutes. Add consomme and wine, stir and cook until thick. Add seasonings, bacon and beef. Simmer covered 1 1/2 hours. Serve over rice. Serves 8 to 10.

MAMA MISTROT'S SWISS STEAK

This was a specialty at my Cajun grandmother's house. When I would go to visit her, she usually made this because she knew I liked it. The gravy was served over rice, of course!

1 round steak, tenderized, and cut into serving pieces
1/2 cup chopped onion
1/2 cup chopped celery
1/4 cup chopped bell pepper
1 (4 ounce) can tomato paste
4 ounces water (use can to measure)
Salt and pepper to taste

Season steak with salt and pepper and brown in small amount of oil until brown. Add vegetables, plus 1 small can tomato paste. Cover and simmer until tender, adding water as needed. Serve over rice.

NEVER FAIL BRISKET

When brisket is on sale, I usually buy a whole one and before freezing, trim it of all the extra fat. The brisket can then be cut in half, if you wish, and wrapped in wax paper and then in foil and frozen. When ready to cook, remove the foil and wax paper (the wax paper keeps the meat from sticking to the foil), replace the foil and proceed as below. This method has never failed to produce a tender, moist brisket. Leftovers can be used to make hash (see the Main Dishes section of this cookbook) or to make a very unusual and delicious Brisket Salad (see the Salads section of this cookbook).

Whole or half brisket, trimmed of all fat
Garlic powder
Salt and pepper

Start with a frozen brisket. Line a roasting pan with foil, with enough foil on all edges to fold over and completely seal the brisket. Rub garlic powder, salt and pepper liberally on all sides of the brisket. Enclose tightly in the foil and double seal the edges so as to keep all the heat and juices inside the foil package. Put in a cold oven, set at 300 degrees and cook 6 to 8 hours until fork tender. Do not unwrap the foil; test for tenderness with a cooking fork after 6 hours. Water may be added to the pan if necessary, but usually it is not necessary. When done, carefully fold back foil and allow to rest 20 to 30 minutes before slicing across the grain.

EXCELLENT BEEF TENDER

*I have made this for years; whenever you want a really
delicious and foolproof meat dish, this is the best!*

1 (6 pound) beef tender (eye of round may also be used)
Salt and pepper

Preheat oven to 500 degrees. Salt and pepper the meat generously, place on a rack in a baking pan and roast 4 to 5 minutes per pound. Turn off the oven and let the roast rest in the oven without opening the door for 1 1/2 to 2 hours. The result is a marvelous rare and tender roast with the juices well distributed. Be sure to use the high oven temperature and your kitchen vent!

MUSHROOM HAMBURGER PATTIES

This really "dresses up" plain hamburger patties!

1 1/2 pounds ground beef
1 can cream of mushroom soup
1/4 cup onion, chopped
1/2 cup breadcrumbs, fine and dry
1 egg, beaten
1/2 teaspoon salt
1/8 teaspoon pepper
1/3 cup water

Mix raw ground beef with 1/4 cup of the undiluted soup and add onion, breadcrumbs, egg, salt and pepper. Be sure to mix thoroughly. Shape into 6 patties and place in baking dish. Bake at 350 degrees for 30 minutes. Remove from oven and spoon off excess grease. Combine remaining soup with water and pour over patties. Return to oven and bake an additional 10 minutes.

Marilyn Zengler

BLACK FOREST BEEF AND ONIONS

The beer adds a wonderful hearty flavor.

3 pounds beef chuck, cubed
8 tablespoons butter
¹/₄ cup flour
¹/₄ cup parsley
1 teaspoon thyme
1 bay leaf
2 tablespoons wine vinegar
2 cups beer
3 onions, sliced
1 teaspoon sugar
Salt and pepper to taste

Flour beef and brown in 4 tablespoons butter. Add parsley, thyme, bay leaf, wine vinegar and beer. Bring to a boil; simmer 1 hour, covered, or until meat is tender. Sauté 3 onions in the rest of the butter; add 1 teaspoon sugar and cook until glazed. Add to beef. Season to taste with 1 teaspoon salt and ¹/₂ teaspoon pepper. Serve over noodles.

COLD ROAST PORK

This is good hot or cold. The caraway seed is an essential ingredient to this recipe and makes it very unusual and elegant. This is a wonderful meat dish to serve at a buffet dinner because the meat is fork tender.

3 ¹/₂ to 4 pound boneless pork shoulder; or 5 ¹/₂ to 6 pound pork loin

2 teaspoons salt

3 to 4 cloves garlic, sliced thin

1 cup coarsely chopped carrots

1 rib celery, chopped

2 onions, skin on, sliced

¹/₂ cup oil

1 teaspoon caraway seed, slightly bruised

10 to 12 black peppercorns, slightly bruised

¹/₂ teaspoon dry marjoram

4 cups water

If you buy a pork loin with bone in, ask butcher to debone it for roasting. Tie boned shoulder or loin with butcher string, or ask butcher to do it. Rub roast with salt and let stand at least 1 hour at room temperature. Preheat oven to 375 degrees. In a roasting pan with a tight-fitting lid, scatter garlic, carrots, celery and onions on bottom. Place pork roast on vegetables. Heat oil in a small saucepan over high heat until it is smoking hot. Sprinkle caraway seed, peppercorns and marjoram on pork and around it on vegetables. Sear surface of meat by ladling or pouring the hot oil over it, turning meat with a large fork so it is evenly seared. Pour 2 cups water in roasting pan and roast, covered, in preheated oven about 45 minutes. Lower heat to 300 degrees and roast 2 more hours, basting every 15 minutes.

Remove cover, turn roast, baste again, and add remaining 2 cups water, pouring it carefully around meat in small amounts so as not to cool pan juices. Continue roasting, uncovered, 30 minutes, basting every 10 minutes and turning after each basting. Remove roast from oven, transfer to a small casserole or loaf pan, strain pan juices over it and let cool at room temperature. While it cools, turn it a couple of times so that no surface will dehydrate. Chill overnight.

The next day, or even after two days, the liquid around the roast will have turned into a gelatin, which you can serve finely chopped next to the meat. Slice the pork as thin as you can and serve with a German-type mustard sauce or with applesauce. Serves 8.

★

PERFECT PORK OR BEEF TENDERLOIN

2 to 3 pound fresh whole pork or beef tenderloin
Celery salt
Lemon pepper
Garlic powder
Cracked black pepper

Spray a 9 $^1/_2$ x 11-inch metal baking pan with non-stick spray. Lay a piece of wax paper long enough to overlap the long side of the pan. Place the tenderloin in the middle of the pan. Coat the meat with spices in the order above, rolling the tenderloin in the wax paper and forming a thin crust on the meat. Remove wax paper. Roast uncovered at 325 degrees for 45 minutes to 1 hour. Allow to cool slightly before slicing into $^3/_4$-inch slices.

ANGELA D. NOBLE

PORK TENDERLOIN WITH RASPBERRY CHIPOTLE SAUCE

I medium pork tenderloin
I bottle Fischer & Wieser Roasted Raspberry Chipotle Sauce
Garlic powder
Salt
Pepper

Season tenderloin to taste with spices. Broil to desired doneness. In small saucepan, warm the Raspberry Chipotle Sauce. Do not boil. When done, slice tenderloin into serving pieces and place on platter. Pour sauce over meat and serve with noodles. Extra sauce may be served on the side.

Fischer & Weiser Specialty Foods
Fredericksburg, Texas

FAVORITE PORK CHOPS

This is so simple and is wonderfully tasty.

4 to 6 rib pork chops, trimmed of all fat
Lawry's seasoned salt
Black pepper
I can cream of mushroom soup

Brown seasoned pork chops on both sides in skillet that has been sprayed with non-stick cooking spray. Pour soup over, turn heat down to low and let simmer for 20 minutes, covered tightly. Stir occasionally to prevent sticking. $^1/_4$ to $^1/_2$ cup water may be added, if necessary. Serve over rice or mashed potatoes.

HAM BOILED DINNER

This is an excellent way to use up the last of a ham. Served with German mustard on the side and a big pan of cornbread, it makes a complete meal.

Ham bone with meat attached
Potatoes, quartered
Carrots, cut in chunks
Cabbage, quartered

Put ham bone in large covered pot with potatoes and carrots. Add water almost to cover. Bring to boil over medium heat and cook about 10 minutes. Add cabbage to top of vegetables and cook about 15 minutes until vegetables are tender but not overdone. Sprinkle with pepper (do not add salt) and dill weed. Lift out vegetables and ham bone and arrange on platter to serve.

VENISON CUBES WITH MUSHROOMS AND GREEN PEPPER

1 pound venison tenderloin, cubed
1 large onion, thinly sliced
Oil
1 pound fresh mushrooms, sliced
2 large green peppers, sliced
Garlic salt, pepper to taste
1 package brown gravy mix

Brown venison and onion in oil in heavy skillet over medium low heat. Add mushrooms and green peppers. Cook slowly until soft. Add garlic, salt and pepper. Prepare gravy mix according to package directions, using 1 cup water. Pour over meat and vegetables. Reduce heat to low; cover. Simmer for 20 minutes or until gravy thickens. Serve over rice.

FRAN STRASSER

EASY DOVE BREASTS

12 dove breasts, skinned
1 package chicken gravy mix
Salt and pepper to taste
1 to 2 tablespoons margarine

Place dove breasts in foil-lined 8x8-inch pan. Sprinkle with gravy mix, salt and pepper; dot with margarine. Drizzle $^1/_3$ to $^1/_2$ cup water over breasts; seal foil tightly. Bake at 350 degrees for one hour.

FRAN STRASSER

HONEY-GLAZED QUAIL

My good friend, Fran Strasser, knows how to cook
all game because her husband, Herb, is a hunter.

8 partially boned quail
Salt and freshly ground pepper
2 tablespoons plus 2 teaspoons unsalted butter
1 tablespoon olive oil
1 tablespoon plus 1 $^1/_2$ teaspoons honey

Rinse and dry the quail. Flatten them gently with the heel of your hand; season lightly with salt and pepper. In a very large skillet, combine 2 tablespoons of the butter with the oil and 2 teaspoons of the honey over moderately high heat. Add the quail, skin side down, and cook until well browned, about 5 minutes. Turn, cover and cook until the juices run clear when the thigh is pierced with a knife, about 5 minutes longer. Arrange 2 quail on each plate. Add 3 tablespoons of water and the remaining 2$^1/_2$ teaspoons honey to the pan and boil until thickened, about 1 minute. Whisk in the remaining 2 teaspoons butter. Season with salt and pepper to taste, spoon over the quail and serve.

FRAN STRASSER

FAVORITE DUCK RECIPE

2 to 3 ducks
Onions, coarsely chopped
Carrots, coarsely chopped
Celery, coarsely chopped
Instant chicken bouillon to taste
1 can cream of mushroom soup
1 package dry stuffing mix, prepared
Chopped apple
Raisins

Wash ducks, wipe dry inside and out. Place ducks, onions, carrots and celery with a small amount of water in large saucepan; add bouillon. Boil until tender. Remove meat from bones, reserve stock. Place duck in greased casserole. Combine soup with reserved stock. Pour over duck. Prepare stuffing mix using package directions. Add additional chopped onion, apple and raisins; mix well. Spread over soup mixture. Bake at 350 degrees for 30 minutes.

FRAN STRASSER

HELPFUL HINT:

A kitchen match dropped into oil being heated in a skillet will burst into flame when frying temperature is reached.

GOOSE IN ORANGE SAUCE

I large **Canada** goose
I envelope brown gravy mix
2 tablespoons sugar
I (6 ounce) can frozen orange juice concentrate, pulp-free
I cup hot water
$^1/_4$ cup flour
2 tablespoons orange marmalade or plum jelly

Slowly thaw the bird (overnight in cold water) and clean thoroughly. Place goose breast down in oven-cooking bag, seal and bake in a covered roasting pan for approximately 1 to 1½ hours in a 325 degree oven. Pour fat and drippings from goose and discard. Mix remaining ingredients together and pour over goose and into cooking bag. Return to roasting pan and continue cooking 2 to 4 more hours, or until goose is falling off bones or appears to be tender. Pour sauce into gravy boat and serve with sliced goose.

FRAN STRASSER

TEX-MEX CHICKEN

*I made up this recipe because I wanted to duplicate one of
my favorite Mexican restaurant's popular chicken dishes.
Easy, good and tasty, it's best served with rice.*

4 chicken breasts
Lawry's seasoned salt
1 small can green chile sauce
¹/₂ cup sour cream

Spray skillet with non-stick cooking spray. Brown chicken breasts
well on both sides; season with Lawry's salt. Cover tightly and cook
on low heat for 20 minutes or until tender. Add green chile sauce,
cover and simmer another 5 minutes. Remove chicken from skillet,
pour green chile sauce over breasts, and top with a dollop of sour
cream.

═══════ ★ ═══════

CHICKEN IN MUSTARD CREAM SAUCE

This sauce is also good prepared with a pork tender or boneless pork chops.

4 boneless skinless chicken breasts
¹/₈ teaspoon pepper
2 tablespoons Dijon mustard
2 tablespoons olive oil
¹/₂ cup evaporated milk or cream
¹/₂ cup white wine
4 teaspoons Dijon mustard
2 teaspoons capers, drained

Flatten chicken breasts to ¹/₄-inch thick between 2 sheets of plastic
wrap. Sprinkle with pepper and spread one side with mustard. Cook

chicken in oil over medium heat for 10 to 15 minutes, turning once. Remove and keep warm. Combine remaining ingredients in skillet and simmer until mixture thickens. Spoon over chicken breasts and serve.

CHICKEN BECHAMEL

Skimmed evaporated milk may be substituted for the cream to make a low-fat version of this dish.

4 large chicken breasts, boned and halved
1 stick butter
1 onion, finely chopped
1 clove garlic
1 to 2 bay leaves
1 can bouillon or consomme
2 small cans mushrooms (stems and pieces), or 8 ounces fresh mushrooms, sliced
$^{1}/_{2}$ to 1 cup white wine
Flour to thicken sauce
$^{1}/_{2}$ pint heavy cream or half-and-half
Salt and red pepper to taste

Melt butter. Brown chicken in butter. Remove to baking pan. Cook onion and garlic in butter until tender, add flour, bouillon, bay leaf, white wine and mushrooms. Simmer slowly until well heated. Add cream or milk, stirring until smooth. Season with salt and red pepper. Pour over chicken and bake at 350 degrees for about 30 minutes. Serve with rice. Sauce, with chicken, may be frozen. Makes 4 servings.

LIME-CILANTRO CHICKEN

This is another good, quick, easy, low-fat chicken dish.

4 chicken breast halves, skinless and boneless
I lime, sliced
I teaspoon Mesquite-seasoned salt
¹/₂ cup cilantro, chopped

Heat a heavy skillet, then coat with cooking spray. Brown breasts on both sides, sprinkling each side with salt before turning. Arrange lime slices on top of chicken, sprinkle cilantro on top and turn heat to medium-low. Cover and cook for 10 minutes, turn, add ¹/₂ cup water, and cook 5 minutes more, covered, until breasts are tender. Serve with rice and black beans.

★

MAMA MISTROT'S SMOTHERED CHICKEN

For Sunday dinner at my grandparents' house, we always had chicken two ways: fried and smothered.

I fryer
¹/₄ cup oil
I cup onions, chopped
¹/₂ cup celery, chopped
¹/₄ cup bell pepper, chopped
¹/₂ cup water

Cut up chicken; brown in hot oil. Then brown vegetables in same pot. Add water and salt and pepper. Cook slowly until tender, adding more water if necessary. Serve with rice or mashed potatoes.

POLLO VERDE

The Gristmill Restaurant's Pollo Verde is one of its most popular entrees.

8 chicken breasts, grilled or poached

Tomatillo Sauce:
3 pounds tomatillos, husked
I cup yellow onions
4 to 6 serrano peppers
¹/₄ teaspoon garlic powder
2 to 3 tablespoons lime juice
3 tablespoons chopped cilantro
2 cups diced avocados

Bean Sauce:
¹/₄ quart pinto beans
I tablespoon cilantro
2 cups bean juice

In food processor, blend all tomatillo sauce ingredients except avocado. Add avocado dices to puréed sauce and chill.

In food processor, purée pinto beans, cilantro and bean juice and heat until hot.

Ladle ¹/₂ cup of hot bean sauce on plate. Place grilled chicken breast on bean sauce. Ladle ¹/₂ cup chilled tomatillo sauce over chicken breast and garnish with serrano pepper.

GRISTMILL RESTAURANT
GRUENE TEXAS

House rules:
this is my house and I make the rules!

SOUTH SEAS CHICKEN

This is a great dish to make when you forgot to take the chicken out of the freezer or when you have unexpected guests, because you start with frozen chicken breasts. If by some lucky chance you have fresh or thawed chicken breasts, bake the dish only 25 minutes before topping with the pineapple. Another good thing about this recipe is that it is seriously low fat!

Non-stick cooking spray
4 skinless, boneless chicken breasts
4 tablespoons soy sauce
2 tablespoons vinegar
2 tablespoons catsup
2 tablespoons packed brown sugar
1 (8 ounce) can) sliced pineapple in its own juice, drained

Heat oven to 375 degrees. Lightly coat a baking dish with cooking spray. Place the frozen chicken breasts in the dish without overlapping them, if possible. In a separate dish, combine the soy sauce, vinegar, catsup and brown sugar. Stir until the sugar dissolves. Pour the sauce mixture over the chicken. Bake for 45 to 50 minutes, turning twice so the meat develops a brown glaze on both sides. Ten minutes before cooking time is up, place one slice of pineapple on top of each chicken breast; bake for 10 minutes longer. Serve with rice or potatoes, passing the cooking sauce on the side. Serves 4.

The table is a meeting place, a gathering ground, the source of sustenance and nourishment, festivity, safety and satisfaction.
—Laurie Colwin

CHICKEN AND DRESSING

This is a wonderful dish to make up and serve for a family or company
supper. When it's not quite time for Thanksgiving or Christmas, and
you just want something homey and flavorful, serve this.

1 (2 ¹/₂ pound) chicken
1 teaspoon onion powder
1 teaspoon celery salt
1 teaspoon salt
¹/₂ teaspoon pepper
1 bay leaf
4 cups water
1 cup celery, sliced
1 medium to large onion, chopped fine
¹/₂ package Pepperidge Farm bread stuffing mix
¹/₂ package Pepperidge Farm cornbread stuffing mix
5 or 6 pieces of stale white bread, or 3 cups trimmed bread
    crusts or leftover stale bread
1 tablespoon sage

In a large pot, bring the chicken, onion powder, celery salt, salt and pepper, bay leaf, and 4 cups water to a boil. Cover pot, turn heat down to simmer and cook for about 45 minutes to 1 hour until chicken is very tender.

Lift the chicken out of the broth and allow the meat to cool until it can be removed from the bones and cut into small pieces. Strain the chicken broth and reserve.

In a large bowl, combine the celery, onion, stuffing mixes and bread. Add the reserved chicken broth, chicken pieces and sage. Stir until the mixture is thoroughly blended. Add more hot water if needed to make a wet dressing, about the consistency of cornbread batter. Adjust the seasoning if needed. Grease a large casserole and pour the dressing mixture into the casserole. Bake at 375 degrees for 45 minutes to 1 hour, just until set and top is nicely browned.

AUNT CECILE'S CHICKEN AND DUMPLINGS

My grandparents, Mama and Papa Mistrot, "took in" Mama's old maid cousin early in their marriage. Aunt Cecile lived with Mama and Papa, did housework and looked after the children, and later the grandchildren, in exchange for room and board. Aunt Cecile was a part of the family and we all loved her, even though she could be somewhat irascible at times. This chicken and dumpling recipe was her contribution to Sunday dinners. The dumplings, because they contain egg, are light, fluffy and golden.

1 frying chicken, cut into pieces
1 cup flour
1 teaspoon salt
¹/₂ teaspoon pepper
¹/₂ cup onion, finely chopped
¹/₂ cup green pepper, finely chopped

DUMPLINGS:
1 cup Bisquick
2 eggs, beaten slightly
³/₄ cup milk
¹/₂ teaspoon salt
¹/₂ teaspoon pepper

Mix the flour, salt and pepper in a plastic bag. Shake the chicken pieces, a few at a time, and brown in a large stewpot in about 2 tablespoons cooking oil. Remove the pieces as they are browned to make room for the other pieces. Do not crowd the chicken and allow to brown thoroughly. Add the onion and green pepper during the last browning process; return all the chicken parts to the pan and add about 2 cups water. Cover, turn heat down to low, and simmer, stirring occasionally, until chicken is done, about 30 minutes. Remove the chicken pieces from the broth and bring the broth to boiling. Up to another cup of water may be added at this point.

Meanwhile, mix the dumpling ingredients. Spoon the dumplings into the boiling broth, one spoon at a time. As the dumplings cook, they will rise to the top of the broth. Remove and keep warm until all the dumpling mixture is used. Return the chicken to the broth, top with dumplings and serve.

CHICKEN ROSEMARY

This makes a flavorful sauce, so serve with rice, noodles or potatoes.

1 fryer cut in parts, or 4 whole chicken breasts
Salt and pepper
$^1/_2$ cup flour with paprika added to taste
Oil
1 chopped onion
1 clove garlic, chopped
1 teaspoon rosemary
$^1/_2$ teaspoon marjoram
2 tablespoons vermouth or white wine
Juice of 1 lemon
1 can cream of mushroom soup

Salt and pepper fryer parts. Dredge in flour/paprika mixture. Brown fryer parts in oil; then saute onions and garlic. Pour off excess oil. Add rest of ingredients. Cover and bake at 325 degrees for 30 to 45 minutes. Serves 4.

MY FRIED CHICKEN

It's very important to use skinless chicken in this recipe; besides having less fat, the batter adheres to the chicken meat itself and makes it very moist and tender.

Skinned cut up chicken parts, or skinned chicken breasts
1 cup buttermilk
1 ½ cups flour
1 teaspoon salt
½ teaspoon pepper

Put chicken pieces in a bowl and cover with buttermilk; turn to coat chicken. Refrigerate until ready to cook. Put the flour and seasonings in a plastic bag and add chicken one piece at a time, shaking to coat. Lay chicken out on a piece of waxed paper while heating oil. In a large heavy skillet (an iron skillet is best) heat about 2 cups oil or shortening until very hot. You can tell it is hot enough when a kitchen match placed in the oil bursts into flame. Remove the match and add chicken pieces one at a time until there is a single layer of chicken in the skillet. DO NOT CROWD THE CHICKEN PIECES. Brown chicken thoroughly, turn over and brown the other side. When both sides are brown, turn heat down low, cover skillet, and cook chicken 10 minutes or so until no blood runs when the pieces are pierced next to the bone. Remove skillet, turn heat back up, and brown, turning once, until dark brown (not burned) and crispy on both sides. Remove chicken pieces and drain on paper towels. Continue to add chicken pieces in this manner until all chicken is cooked.

Gravy: Pour off all except about ⅓ cup of the frying grease, retaining any crispy bits of chicken or batter in the pan. Add about ¼ cup flour, stir and brown over medium low heat until very brown but not burned. Meanwhile, mix 1 cup milk and 1 cup water. Add the milk-water mixture to the browned flour, stirring constantly over low heat, until the gravy is thickened. Correct seasoning to taste.

SALTGRASS TRAIL MARINATED CHICKEN BREASTS

1 cup Kraft Italian dressing
1 ½ cups cottonseed oil
1 (12 ounce) can papaya juice
½ cup Lawry's dry Italian dressing mix
¼ cup Lawry's seasoned salt
1 tablespoon black pepper
¼ cup soy sauce
2 minced garlic cloves
1 jalapeno
8 boneless, skinless chicken breasts
½ bunch cilantro

First, mince 2 cloves of garlic and remove the seeds and stem from the jalapeno. Next, place the Kraft Italian dressing, cottonseed oil, papaya juice, Lawry's dry Italian dressing mix, Lawry's seasoned salt, black pepper, soy sauce, garlic and jalapeno into a blender and mix for approximately 30 minutes, until emulsified. Mix the chicken and emulsified mixture together, then chop the cilantro and add to the mix. Mix all ingredients well and allow to marinate for 24 hours before use. Grill the marinated chicken breasts over mesquite for a great flavor.

SALTGRASS STEAKHOUSE
HOUSTON, DALLAS AND
SAN ANTONIO, TEXAS

GRANNY'S CHICKEN BREAST

*This is one of Tammy's Granny's favorite low
fat recipes and it's really easy and good.*

Chicken Breasts
Crushed Corn Flakes
Milk
Salt and pepper to taste

Remove any skin or fat from chicken. Salt and pepper chicken, dip
in milk then roll in corn flakes and place on a lightly greased cookie
sheet in 350 degree oven to bake about 1 hour or until done.

TAMMY HUNTER

★

OVEN CRISP CHICKEN

.2 envelopes onion dip mix
1 cup soft breadcrumbs
1 teaspoon salt
¹/₈ teaspoon pepper
2 broiler-fryers, cut up (about 3 pounds each) or
     8 chicken breasts

Combine dip mix, breadcrumbs, salt and pepper in a plastic bag.
Shake chicken pieces, a few at a time, in mixture to coat well. Place,
not touching, in a single layer in a well-buttered, large shallow baking pan. Bake in a moderate (350 degrees) oven for 1 hour or until
tender and richly browned.

STUFFED CRAB

1 pound Alaskan King Crab meat, finely chopped
12 slices of day-old bread
4 tablespoons butter or margarine
2 tablespoons green bell pepper, minced
4 tablespoons fresh green onion, chopped
4 tablespoons celery with leaves, chopped
1 teaspoon salt
$^1/_2$ teaspoon black pepper
2 large eggs, well beaten
1 cup buttermilk
1 cup cracker crumbs

In bowl, sprinkle crab meat over coarsely torn bread. In small saucepan, melt butter and sauté onion, bell pepper and celery until golden brown and tender. Pour vegetable mixture over crab meat and bread. Mix thoroughly with hands. Add salt, pepper and eggs. Mix well and set in refrigerator until cool. Stuff mixture into 6 or 8 clean crab shells. Dip in buttermilk and dredge in cracker crumbs. Bake at 400 degrees for 25 minutes or until golden brown. Serve hot with tartar sauce, if desired.

Note: If you don't have crab shells, Crab Balls can be made from this recipe as follows: shape crab mixture into golf-ball size portions. Dip balls in buttermilk and roll in cracker crumbs. Fry in deep, hot fat (375 degrees) until golden brown. Drain on paper towels. Crab balls can be frozen BEFORE frying. Defrost 4 to 5 hours in refrigerator, then cook as directed.

THE TIMMERMANN SISTERS
GERONIMO, TEXAS

If it walks out of the fridge, let it go!

SOUTHWESTERN STYLE CRAB CAKES WITH LIME AND CHILIES

1 large egg
2 tablespoons mayonnaise, creme fraiche, or sour cream
2 teaspoons Dijon mustard
Pinch of cayenne pepper
$1/2$ teaspoon freshly ground white pepper
Pinch of salt
$1/4$ teaspoon Worcestershire sauce
1 pound fresh or pasteurized precooked crab meat,
    hump or back fin, flaked
$1/4$ cup chopped parsley
$1/4$ cup chopped green onions
8 to 10 saltine crackers, crushed or 1 cup soft white
    breadcrumbs
1 to 2 fresh 2-inch serrano chilies, seeded and minced
2 tablespoons unsalted sweet butter
2 tablespoons vegetable oil
Lime wedges, for garnish

Mix together the egg, mayonnaise, mustard, pepper, salt and Worcestershire sauce. Add the crab meat, parsley, green onions, saltine crackers and chilies. Mix thoroughly. Shape and press the mixture into 10 or 12 round patties, place on foil, cover, and chill for at least $1/2$ hour before cooking. The recipe can be prepared ahead and refrigerated for 5 to 6 hours. Bring to room temperature before using. Heat the butter and oil in a skillet. Add crab cakes and sauté on both sides over medium-high heat a few minutes or until golden and lightly crispy. Drain on paper towels. Serve hot with lime wedges.

GAIDO'S OF GALVESTON SHRIMP CREOLE

*A P. T. A. mom shared this wonderful recipe by preparing
this dish for a "Teacher's Appreciation Luncheon."*

2 pounds fresh shrimp
2 tablespoons lemon juice
2 tablespoons Worcestershire sauce
2 teaspoons salt
3 tablespoons butter
1 medium onion, chopped
¹/₂ bell pepper, chopped
2 cloves garlic, minced
2 tablespoons flour
1 teaspoon sugar
¹/₄ teaspoon pepper
2 ¹/₄ cups tomatoes
1 (8 ounce) can tomato sauce

Soak shelled shrimp in lemon juice, Worcestershire and salt. Melt
butter and add onion, bell pepper, and garlic; saute for 5 minutes.
Blend flour, sugar and pepper into vegetable mixture. Combine tomatoes and tomato sauce with the above mixture. Simmer covered
over low heat for 15 to 20 minutes. Add shrimp and juice and cook
5 minutes. Serve over hot buttered rice.

PAT FRASE

Flops are part of life's menu and I'm never a girl to miss out on a course.
—Rosalind Russell

RICE SHRIMP PARTY PIE

This can be made up to one day ahead and refrigerated until time to bake.

Crust:
2 tablespoons parsley
2 tablespoons pimiento
1 tablespoon onion
¼ teaspoon salt
⅛ teaspoon pepper
2 tablespoons butter
3 cups hot rice

Filling:
1 ½ pounds cleaned raw shrimp
2 tablespoons butter
1 can cream of mushroom soup
1 tablespoon lemon juice
¼ teaspoon cayenne

Chop vegetables finely and mix with seasonings and butter into hot rice. Press evenly around sides and top of 10-inch pie pan. Brown shrimp in butter and place in rice shell. Mix rest of ingredients in same skillet. Pour over shrimp. Bake at 350 degrees for 30 minutes. Serves 4 to 6.

SHRIMP TARRAGON WITH PIMIENTO RICE

This is a nice dish for a party. It can be made ahead,
then reheated briefly just before assembling and serving.

6 tablespoons butter
9 tablespoons flour
4 cans cream of shrimp soup
1 ¹/₂ cups chicken broth
6 tablespoons lemon juice
1 ¹/₂ teaspoons tarragon
2 teaspoons dried onion
Salt and pepper
4 pounds shrimp, shelled and cooked

In large pot over low heat, melt butter; blend flour in and cook 2 to 3 minutes, but do not brown. Blend in soup, broth and seasonings. Add shrimp and cook 5 to 10 minutes until heated through.

PIMIENTO RICE

1 large chopped onion
1 stick butter
1 (7 ounce) jar diced pimiento
2 ¹/₂ cups rice
5 ¹/₂ cups water
1 teaspoon salt

Bring water to a boil, add salt and rice. Bring to a boil again, stir, cover and simmer on very low heat 20 minutes until water is absorbed. Turn off heat. Meanwhile, sauté onion in butter and mix with pimiento. When rice is done, mix with the onion and pimiento. Serve shrimp over rice. Serves 12.

RONNIE'S MOM'S SHRIMP

This is spicy, messy and delicious. Everyone peels their own!

3 pounds shrimp, rinsed but not shelled
3 sticks butter
6 tablespoons Worcestershire sauce
1 ¹/₂ teaspoons garlic powder
1 teaspoon salt
4 tablespoons lemon juice
¹/₂ teaspoon cayenne pepper
2 tablespoons rosemary

Heat oven to 350 degrees. In a large flat baking pan, while the oven is heating, melt the butter; stir in the spices and mix. When the oven is at the correct temperature, add the shrimp to the pan and bake 20 minutes until shrimp is done, turning several times to baste in the sauce. Serve with lots of napkins and good French bread.

SOLE, SHRIMP AND LOBSTER

2 pounds sole or flounder fillets
2 cans cream of shrimp soup
1 cup cooked shrimp, crab or lobster
2 tablespoons Parmesan cheese
1 tablespoon butter
1 tablespoon vermouth or white wine, thickened with
   ¹/₂ tablespoon flour

Place fillets in shallow, buttered pan. Blend flour/vermouth mixture into soup. Spread soup over fillets, concealing shrimp pieces under fish. Sprinkle cheese over all and dot with butter. Bake 30 minutes at 375 degrees. Add other seafood on top and bake 5 minutes more. Serves 6.

BRONZE CATFISH WITH TEQUILA SAUCE

8 catfish fillets
McCormick's Cajun seasoning
Limes

TEQUILA SAUCE

2 sticks butter, softened
2 tablespoons tequila
1 clove fresh garlic
Salt and pepper to taste
2 tablespoons chopped cilantro
Dash of lemon juice

Combine all ingredients for Tequila Sauce and mix well. Refrigerate until ready for use. Season catfish fillets with McCormick's Cajun seasoning; grill or sauté until done. Top with one tablespoon of tequila butter and a squeeze of lime.

GRISTMILL RESTAURANT
GRUENE TEXAS

SANTA FE FISH

*This is a healthy, tasty fish recipe. I usually
serve it with saffron rice and black beans.*

1 pound fish fillets
Juice of 1 lime
Salt and pepper
¹/₂ to ³/₄ cup salsa

Preheat oven to 375 degrees. Spray glass dish with non-stick cooking spray. Lay fish in a single layer. Pour lime juice, salt and pepper over fish. Turn fish to coat; spoon on salsa. Bake 10 to 15 minutes. Serves 4.

★

PECAN CATFISH THAT BITES BACK!

*D. L. Jardine's Blazin' Saddle Hot Sauce and other Jardine
products are available at the Gruene General Store.*

¹/₄ cup dry breadcrumbs
³/₄ cup finely chopped pecans
6 (6 to 8 ounce) boned, skinned catfish fillets
¹/₄ cup D. L. Jardine's Blazin' Saddle Hot Sauce
¹/₂ cup butter

Put the breadcrumbs and pecans into a food processor and pulse until the pecans are finely ground. Coat the fillets with D. L. Jardine's Blazin' Saddle Hot Sauce, then roll catfish in the pecan mixture. Melt the butter or margarine in a frying pan. Fry the fish over medium heat until it is cooked through and the pecan crust is golden brown (approximately 3 minutes on each side). For those who prefer the hotter side of hot, top cooked fish with more Blazin' Saddle Hot Sauce.

Jardine Foods of Texas

FRIED CATFISH FINGERS

*McIlhenny's Tabasco brand pepper sauce can
be found at the Gruene General Store.*

¹/₂ cup lemon juice
2 teaspoons Tabasco pepper sauce
1 ¹/₂ pounds catfish fillets, cut crosswise into ³/₄-inch strips
²/₃ cup yellow cornmeal
²/₃ cup flour
2 teaspoons salt
1 quart vegetable oil (approximately)

In a large bowl stir together lemon juice and Tabasco sauce. Add fish; toss to coat well. Cover; marinate 1 hour. In shallow dish, stir together cornmeal, flour and salt. Pour oil into heavy 3-quart saucepan or deep fryer, filling no more than ¹/₃ full. Heat over medium heat to 350 degrees. Coat fish with cornmeal mixture; shake off excess. Carefully add to oil, a few at a time. Cook 2 minutes or until golden. Drain on paper towels. Serve with Quick and Sassy Bayou Dip or Tabasco Picante Sauce, if desired. Makes 6 to 8 appetizer servings.

MCILHENNY COMPANY
TABASCO BRAND PRODUCTS

May all your weeds be wildflowers.

PEPPERED FISH WITH CREAMY DILL SAUCE

4 fish fillets, any kind (cod, snapper, flounder or catfish are good)
2 teaspoons olive oil, divided
2 tablespoons coarsely ground pepper
Vegetable cooking spray
2 cups hot cooked rice
Creamy Dill Sauce

Brush fish on both sides with 1 teaspoon olive oil; sprinkle with pepper; gently press into fish. Cover and let stand 15 minutes. Coat a large non-stick skillet with cooking spray, add remaining 1 teaspoon olive oil, place over medium heat. Cook fillets on both sides, for 3 to 5 minutes or until fish flakes easily. Remove from heat and keep warm. Spoon rice onto serving plate, top with fish fillet and sauce. Serves 4.

CREAMY DILL SAUCE
This is fast, easy and low fat.

1 (10 ounce) container refrigerated reduced-calorie
Alfredo sauce
2 tablespoons dry white wine
1 teaspoon dried dill weed

Combine all ingredients for Dill Sauce in saucepan; cook, stirring constantly, over medium heat until heated (or microwave, covered, 1 to 2 minutes). Remove from heat and keep warm.

TUNA ST. JACQUES

This is a good luncheon or light supper dish.

2 green onions, chopped fine
¹/₄ cup finely chopped mushrooms
2 tablespoons butter
2 tablespoons flour
Pepper
²/₃ cup strong chicken broth
¹/₄ cup vermouth or white wine
I can tuna, drained
2 tablespoons parsley
2 tablespoons butter
¹/₄ cup cracker crumbs
I tablespoon Parmesan cheese
Lemon wedges

Sauté vegetables in butter; stir in flour, broth and white wine to make a sauce. Add tuna and parsley. Spoon into buttered shells or individual casserole dishes. Melt 2 tablespoons butter, add crumbs and cheese and top the shells with the crumb mixture. Bake at 450 degrees for 12 minutes. Serves 2. May be doubled or tripled.

SALMON CROQUETTES

1 pound can salmon (do not drain)
$^1/_2$ cup biscuit mix
$^1/_4$ cup chopped green onion
1 egg, beaten
$^1/_2$ teaspoon Worcestershire sauce

Flake fish with a fork, mashing the soft bones. Add other ingredients and mix. Add oil to skillet to $^1/_2$-inch depth and heat until hot. Drop salmon mixture by tablespoons and fry until brown.

WILLIE'S FAVORITE SALMON CAKES

2 eggs, beaten
1 tablespoon lemon juice
1 teaspoon Dijon mustard
1 cup breadcrumbs
1 stalk celery, finely chopped
1 tablespoon grated onion
1 teaspoon dill
$^1/_2$ teaspoon salt
Dash cayenne pepper
1 (15 ounce) can red salmon, with liquid
1 cup finely chopped pecans
1 cup vegetable oil
Lemon wedges and parsley to garnish

Mix together eggs, lemon juice and mustard. Add breadcrumbs, celery, onion, dill and cayenne pepper. Mix well. Add salmon and juice. Form into small patties and roll in finely chopped pecans. Heat oil in a heavy skillet. Cook patties on both sides until lightly browned. Serve with lemon wedges and parsley. Serves 4 to 6.

THE STAFF OF LIFE

Remember that slap-slap-slap of the screen door in the summertime? Remember the smell of biscuits baking for breakfast or supper? Remember an ice-cold glass of lemonade when you were hot and thirsty? Relive all these memories at every turn inside the Gruene General Store where sights, sounds and smells take you back to the good old days.

The walls inside the Gruene General Store are covered with antique and reproduction advertising signs from days gone by. The connoisseur of nostalgia will have a feast of the senses, enjoy-

ing the bounty of old and new items, some for sale and some for display only. Many of the antique fixtures display new or reproduction merchandise. The store has been featured in numerous television commercials and has been the subject of many travel articles in both regional and national publications.

ALLENE'S PANCAKES

This is Jill's sister-in-law's recipe and has been a family favorite for years!

2 ³/₄ cups flour
2 tablespoons baking powder
2 tablespoons sugar
1 teaspoon salt
2 eggs
2 ¹/₂ cups milk
6 tablespoons oil

Sift together the flour, baking powder, sugar and salt. Add the eggs, milk and oil, and mix thoroughly. Pour ¹/₂ cup batter on hot griddle. Turn when holes pop through the wet batter.

JILL KNEUPER

★

RENE'S FLUFFY FLAPJACKS

This was a favorite breakfast food served by Marilyn's mother, Rene Waddle. These pancakes are extra special.

1 ¹/₄ cups flour
2 teaspoons baking powder
¹/₂ teaspoon baking soda
1 cup buttermilk
1 tablespoon sugar
¹/₂ teaspoon salt
2 tablespoons butter, melted
1 beaten egg

In a large mixing bowl, beat 1 egg; add buttermilk, soda, salt, sugar and baking powder. Add melted butter, then add flour. Stir only until flour is moistened. Batter will be lumpy and thick. Cook on ungreased griddle (or electric skillet at 400 degrees). Flip when surface loses its shine. Flip just once if possible.

BOB AND MARILYN KEYS

CREPE CAKES

The McCaskill's breakfasts at Gruene Mansion Inn are famous.

2 cups all-purpose flour
2 tablespoons baking powder
2 tablespoons sugar
1 teaspoon salt
2 cups milk
2 eggs
¹/₃ cup oil
1 (21 ounce) can blueberry pie filling
1 (16 ounce) can blueberries in syrup
1 teaspoon lemon juice
Whipped cream

In a large bowl, sift the flour, baking powder, sugar and salt together 3 times. In a separate bowl combine the milk, eggs and oil and beat until frothy. Pour the liquids into the flour mixture and beat with a wire whisk until smooth. To cook, preheat a cast-iron griddle over medium heat until the griddle begins to smoke. Spray the griddle with cooking spray. Spoon the batter onto the hot griddle. When "holes" appear all through the pancakes, they are ready to turn. Cook about 30 seconds each side. Remove and keep warm.

In a saucepan, combine the pie filling, blueberries in syrup and lemon juice. Heat over medium heat until bubbly. Serve steaming hot over pancakes and top with a dollop of whipped cream. Makes 4 to 5 servings. The batter stays fresh in the refrigerator for 4 to 5 days.

SHARON AND BILL MCCASKILL
GRUENE MANSION INN
GRUENE TEXAS

APPLESAUCE BREAD

1 package yeast
2 ¼ cups bread flour
¾ cup wheat flour
½ teaspoon salt
½ cup Aspen Mulling Spices
⅔ cup warm applesauce
1 tablespoon butter, room temperature
½ cup warm apple juice
½ cup grated fresh apple

Mix together dry ingredients. Add to mixture of applesauce, butter, apple juice and grated apple. Hand knead and let the dough rise until it is double in size. Punch it down, divide into two portions, and place each in a 8x4-inch loaf pan. Let rise until double in size again. Bake at 350 degrees until brown 40 to 45 minutes.

ASPEN MULLING SPICE
ASPEN, COLORADO

SAUSAGE BREAD

1 cup raisins
1 pound "hot" bulk country sausage
1 ½ cups brown sugar
1 ½ cups granulated sugar
2 eggs
1 cup pecans, chopped
3 cups flour
1 teaspoon ground ginger
1 teaspoon pumpkin pie spice
1 teaspoon baking powder
1 cup cold coffee
1 teaspoon baking soda

Simmer raisins in enough water to cover for 5 minutes and drain. Mix sausage, sugars and eggs together. Stir in nuts and raisins. Mix flour, spices and baking powder together. Stir baking soda into coffee. Blend coffee mixture and flour mixture into sausage mixture. Pour into a greased and floured 9-inch tube pan. Bake at 350 degrees for 1 1/2 hours. Serve with cream cheese.

THE TIMMERMANN SISTERS
GERONIMO, TEXAS

★

PUMPKIN BREAD

Aspen Mulling Spice is available at the Gruene General Store.

1 cup oil
3 cups sugar
3 eggs
1 can pumpkin
1/2 teaspoon baking powder
2 1/2 tablespoons Aspen Mulling Spice
1/2 teaspoon baking soda
2 cups white flour
2 cups whole wheat flour
1 teaspoon vanilla
1 cup pecans

Cream sugar and oil. Add eggs and pumpkin. Sift all dry ingredients and stir into pumpkin mix. Add vanilla and pecans. Pour in three small loaf pans (greased and floured). Bake 1 hour 20 minutes at 350 degrees.

ASPEN MULLING SPICE
ASPEN, COLORADO

CRANBERRY BREAD

This bread is delicious, and is great for either dessert or a breakfast/brunch.

2 cups sifted flour
$^1/_2$ teaspoon salt
1 tablespoon melted shortening
1 $^1/_2$ teaspoons baking powder
$^1/_2$ teaspoon baking soda
1 cup sugar
$^1/_2$ cup chopped nuts
1 beaten egg
$^1/_2$ cup orange juice
2 tablespoons hot water
1 cup halved cranberries

Sift dry ingredients together. Combine egg, shortening, orange juice and water and add to dry ingredients. Stir in nuts and cranberries. Grease bottom only of 9x5-inch loaf pan. Bake 70 minutes at 325 degrees. Remove from pan, brush with melted butter. Wrap while hot in wax paper and refrigerate 3 hours.

JILL KNEUPER

DATE STREUSEL MUFFINS

1 egg
2 $^1/_3$ cups Bisquick, divided
1 cup non-fat plain yogurt
$^2/_3$ cup sugar, divided
2 tablespoons vegetable oil
1 teaspoon cinnamon, divided
1 (8 ounce) package chopped dates
2 tablespoons butter

Beat egg in medium bowl. Stir in 2 cups Bisquick, yogurt, $^1/_3$ cup sugar, oil and $^1/_2$ teaspoon cinnamon. Stir just until moistened. Fold in dates. Spoon batter into greased or paper-lined muffin cups. Combine remaining Bisquick, sugar, cinnamon and butter with a fork or pastry blender until crumbly. Sprinkle over top of muffins. Bake at 400 degrees for 15 to 18 minutes or until lightly browned.

OAT BRAN MUFFINS

These are low fat and good for you — delicious, too!

2 cups oat bran cereal, uncooked
$^1/_4$ cup firmly packed brown sugar
2 teaspoons baking powder
$^1/_2$ teaspoon salt
1 cup low-fat milk
2 egg whites, slightly beaten
$^1/_4$ cup honey or molasses
2 tablespoons vegetable oil

Heat oven to 425 degrees. Line 12 medium muffin cups with paper baking cups. Combine dry ingredients; mix well. Add combined milk, egg whites, honey and oil; mix just until dry ingredients are moistened. Fill prepared muffin cups $^3/_4$ full. Bake 15 to 17 minutes until toothpick inserted in center comes out clean and tops are brown.

MY FAVORITE CINNAMON ROLLS

This recipe from one of New Braunfels' old German families is very special.

¹/₂ cup warm milk
¹/₂ cup sugar
1 ¹/₂ teaspoons salt
¹/₄ cup (¹/₂ stick) margarine
¹/₂ cup warm water
2 packages yeast
2 eggs (beaten)
4 ¹/₂ cups unsifted flour
Cinnamon, sugar and raisins (optional)

Scald milk, stir in sugar, salt and margarine in medium sized bowl. Cool mixture to lukewarm temperature. Measure warm water into large bowl. Sprinkle or crumble in yeast; stir until dissolved. Stir in contents of medium sized bowl, eggs and 2¹/₄ cups flour. Beat until smooth. Stir in remaining flour to make a slightly stiff dough. Turn dough on lightly floured board. Knead until smooth and elastic (about 8 minutes). Cover, place in warm place until dough has doubled in size (1 hour).

Turn out dough on a lightly floured board and stretch dough into a rectangular shape approximately ¹/₂-inch thick. Brush dough with margarine, sprinkle with sugar, cinnamon and raisins as desired. Roll dough lengthwise, cutting into 1¹/₂-inch slices. Place slices, sides touching, in greased pan. Place pan in warm place for 15 minutes while dough continues to rise. Bake at 350 degrees for 20 to 25 minutes. Remove from oven and glaze as desired.

ADELINE MAE HARTMANN

★

Marriage is like a garden; it takes a lot of love and a little work each day.

AMARETTO, PEACH AND PECAN COFFEE CAKE

1 cup butter, softened
2 cups sugar
2 large eggs
1 teaspoon vanilla
2 cups flour
1/4 teaspoon salt
1 teaspoon baking powder
1 (8 ounce) carton sour cream
1 cup chopped pecans
1 jar D. L. Jardine's Amaretto, Peach and Pecan Preserves

Beat butter at medium speed with electric mixer for 2 minutes or until creamy. Gradually add sugar, beating at medium speed for 5 to 7 minutes. Add eggs one at a time, beating just until yellow disappears. Stir in vanilla extract. Combine flour, salt and baking powder. Add to butter mixture alternately with sour cream, beginning and ending with flour mixture. Mix at low speed after each addition just until blended. Place about 1/3 batter into greased and floured 12-cup bundt pan. Sprinkle with 1/2 cup pecans and dot with 1/2 jar Amaretto, Peach and Pecan jelly. Top with remaining batter. Sprinkle with remaining pecans and dot with remaining Amaretto, Peach and Pecan jelly. Bake at 350 degrees for 50 to 55 minutes or until wooden pick inserted into cake comes out clean. Cool in pan on wire rack for 10 to 15 minutes. Remove from pan and allow to cool completely on wire rack.

JARDINE FOODS OF TEXAS

CARAMEL-NUT COFFEECAKE

Cake:
1 package white pudding-in-the-mix cake mix
$^1/_2$ cup flour
$^1/_4$ cup oil
$^2/_3$ cup water
2 eggs

Topping:
1 cup packed brown sugar
$^3/_4$ cup chopped nuts
$^1/_4$ cup melted butter or margarine

Preheat oven to 350 degrees. For cake, measure out 1 cup dry cake mix; set aside for topping. Combine remaining cake mix, flour, oil, water and eggs in large mixer bowl. Beat 2 minutes at medium speed. Pour into a greased and floured 13x9x2-inch pan. For topping, combine reserved cake mix, brown sugar and nuts in a small bowl. Add melted butter and mix thoroughly; mixture will be crumbly. Sprinkle on top of batter in pan. Cut through batter with knife to create a marbled effect. Bake at 350 degrees for 30 to 35 minutes. Drizzle glaze over cake.

GLAZE

1 cup powdered sugar
1 tablespoon corn syrup
1 to 2 tablespoons water

Combine sugar, corn syrup and water to reach desired consistency.

JILL KNEUPER

STREUSEL COFFEE CAKE

1 ³/₄ cup Bisquick
³/₄ cup milk
¹/₄ cup sugar
1 tablespoon margarine, melted
1 egg

Topping:
¹/₃ cup packed brown sugar
¹/₂ teaspoon ground cinnamon

Heat oven to 375 degrees. Grease a round 9-inch cake pan. Mix streusel topping ingredients and set aside. Stir Bisquick with milk, sugar, margarine and egg just until blended. Spread in pan and sprinkle with topping. Bake 18 to 23 minutes or until brown. Cut in pie-shaped wedges to serve.

CZECH KOLACHES

1 cup scalded milk
$^{1}/_{3}$ cup sugar
$^{1}/_{4}$ cup warm water
1 package of yeast
$^{1}/_{2}$ cup oil
1 egg
2 egg yolks
1 teaspoon salt
4 to 5 cups flour

Combine yeast and 1/4 cup of water. Let stand for about 15 minutes. Stir well before adding to mixture. Mix together milk, sugar, salt, oil and eggs. Add yeast mixture. Then add 2 cups of flour and mix well. Keep dough as soft as possible. Thick dough does not stay soft when baked. Let rise for about 30 minutes. Add remaining flour and knead well. Cover and let rise in a warm place until double in size. Make into kolaches or rolls.

To make kolaches: Pat dough out onto a greased cookie sheet. Cut into 6-inch squares, add a spoonful of filling and fold up 2 points to the center into kolache shape. Bake at 400 degrees for 10 to 15 minutes. Remove from oven, brush with butter, and sprinkle with sugar.

Note: Fillings must be placed inside or outside of kolache before baking.

CHEESE FILLING

1 pound cottage cheese
1 $^{1}/_{2}$ cups sugar
3 tablespoons melted butter
2 eggs
$^{1}/_{2}$ teaspoon lemon rind
Pinch salt

Combine all ingredients and mix well.

APRICOT FILLING

1 pound cooked apricots
2 to 2 1/2 cups sugar
2 tablespoons melted butter

Combine all ingredients and mix well.

PINEAPPLE FILLING

1 can crushed pineapple
2 tablespoons melted butter
1 cup sugar
2 tablespoons cornstarch

Heat pineapple until it starts to boil. Add mixture of sugar and cornstarch and cook until it thickens. Remove from heat. Add butter and cool before using.

PRUNE FILLING

1 pound cooked prunes
1 1/2 cups sugar
1 teaspoon cinnamon
3 tablespoons melted butter
1 teaspoon vanilla

Combine all ingredients and mix well.

POPPY SEED FILLING

2 cups ground poppy seed
1 cup boiling milk
2 tablespoons cornstarch
1 teaspoon vanilla

Combine all ingredients except for vanilla and cook slowly until mixture thickens. Add vanilla. Let cool.

CONCETTA CHILEK

OLYMPIC LIGHTS BLUEBERRY SCONES

2 cups flour
2 tablespoons sugar
2 teaspoons baking powder
¹/₂ teaspoon baking soda
¹/₂ teaspoon salt
6 tablespoons cold butter
¹/₂ cup frozen blueberries
2 eggs
¹/₂ cup buttermilk, half-and-half, or heavy cream

In large bowl, sift together flour, sugar, baking powder, baking soda and salt. Cut in butter. Stir in blueberries. In small bowl, beat together the eggs and buttermilk. Combine dry and wet ingredients. Mix as little as possible. Turn dough onto floured surface. Pat into ¹/₂-inch thick round and cut into 12 scones. Brush with buttermilk and sprinkle with sugar. Place on ungreased cookie sheet. Bake in top ¹/₃ of 450 degree oven for 12 minutes.

Note: Instead of blueberries, ¹/₂ cup diced dry apricots can be used. If using apricots, add one tablespoon of apricot preserves to the buttermilk. Brush the tops and sprinkle with sugar.

OLYMPIC LIGHTS BED & BREAKFAST
FRIDAY HARBOR, WA

If Mama ain't happy, ain't nobody happy!

HARPER'S CORN BREAD

*This was the recipe of my stepfather, Harper Nixon. It is
the best and easiest cornbread recipe I have ever found.*

¹/₂ **cup flour**
1 cup stone ground cornmeal (yellow)
1 teaspoon salt
1 teaspoon soda
1 teaspoon sugar
1 cup buttermilk
1 egg

Mix all dry ingredients together. Add buttermilk and egg. Spray
two small iron skillets or 2 iron cornbread molds with vegetable
cooking spray and heat in 450 degree oven until hot. Spoon batter
into hot pans and bake 10 to 12 minutes until toothpick inserted in
center tests done. Leftovers, if any, may be frozen and reheated.

MEXICAN CORNBREAD

1 ¹/₃ cups cornmeal mix
2 eggs
¹/₃ **cup oil**
1 cup sour cream, cream or buttermilk
1 cup creamed corn
1 small can green chilies
1 cup sharp cheddar cheese

Mix all ingredients in order given and pour into a 9x9-inch greased
pan. Bake at 325 degrees for one hour.

CONNIE CONE

BEER BREAD

You can't find a recipe any easier than this one!

3 cups self-rising flour
2 tablespoons sugar
I can beer (room temperature)

Mix all ingredients together in a bowl, knead a little, and put in a greased 9x5-inch loaf pan. Bake at 350 degrees for 1 hour.

PAT TEPE

CRUSTY DROP BISCUITS

For a quick breakfast, take some of these out of the freezer and while thawing, fry 1 pound of sausage in a skillet until crumbly; drain grease, add flour and brown for a minute. Add milk to make gravy. Serve sausage gravy with biscuits.

6³/₄ cups flour
I tablespoon salt
3 tablespoons sugar
3 tablespoons baking powder
2 sticks plus 5 tablespoons butter
2¹/₂ cups 1% buttermilk
I egg, beaten
2 tablespoons milk

Mix with your fingers: flour, salt, sugar, baking powder and butter until the consistency of coarse oatmeal. Fold in buttermilk with rubber spatula. Do NOT pat. Drop on cookie sheet. Brush tops with egg and milk mixture. Bake 12 minutes at 425 degrees. Freezes well (thaw, then 425 degrees for 5 minutes). 48 biscuits.

GARLANDA MELTON

ANGEL BISCUITS

5 cups self-rising flour
¼ cup sugar
1 cup shortening
1 package dry yeast
2 tablespoons water
1 teaspoon soda
1 teaspoon salt
2 cups buttermilk

Sift dry ingredients; cut in shortening with a pastry blender. Stir in buttermilk and yeast. Mix well. Pat out gently on waxed paper and cut into biscuits. Bake at 450 degrees for 25 minutes. The dough may be kept in a covered container in the refrigerator for a week and used as needed.

BUTTERMILK BISCUITS

4 cups flour
2 teaspoons salt
4 teaspoons baking powder
4 tablespoons sugar
1 teaspoon baking soda
10 tablespoons butter
1 ½ cups buttermilk

Sift together into a very large bowl the flour, salt, baking powder, sugar and baking soda. Cut in the butter. Lightly mix in the buttermilk. Knead dough together and pat dough ½-inch thick. Cut out biscuits with heart-shaped cookie cutter. Bake in top ⅓ of 450 degree oven for 10 to 12 minutes. Yield: 24 (2-inch) heart biscuits

OLYMPIC LIGHTS BED & BREAKFAST
FRIDAY HARBOR, WA

FAVORITE BUTTERMILK BISCUITS

Bob makes these biscuits as a special weekend breakfast treat.

2 cups flour
1 tablespoon baking powder
¹/₂ teaspoon salt
¹/₂ teaspoon cream of tartar
2 teaspoons sugar (optional)
¹/₂ cup shortening
³/₄ cup buttermilk
¹/₂ teaspoon baking soda

Combine flour, baking powder, salt, cream of tartar and sugar, mixing well. Cut in shortening until mixture resembles coarse meal. Combine buttermilk and baking soda. Add to flour mixture and stir until dry ingredients are moistened. Turn dough out on a lightly floured surface; knead lightly 10 or 12 times. Roll dough to ¹/₂-inch thickness; cut with 2³/₄-inch biscuit cutter. Place on lightly greased baking sheet. Bake at 450 degrees for 10 minutes or until golden brown. Yield: 10 biscuits.

BOB AND MARILYN KEYS

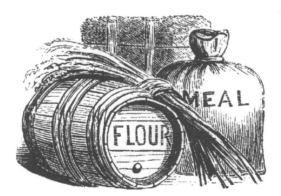

REFRIGERATOR YEAST ROLLS

2 tablespoons active dry yeast
$^1/_3$ cup very warm water
$^1/_2$ cup butter
1 cup milk
4 $^1/_4$ to 4 $^3/_4$ cups unsifted unbleached flour, divided
$^1/_3$ cup sugar
2 teaspoons salt
3 large eggs, room temperature
Oil
Melted butter

Dissolve yeast in warm water. Set aside. In small saucepan over low heat, melt butter in milk. In large bowl, combine 2$^1/_4$ cups flour, sugar, salt, eggs, dissolved yeast and warm milk-butter mixture. Beat with wooden spoon for about 3 minutes. (This step can be done in a food processor using a plastic blade.) Add remaining flour by hand. The dough will be soft and sticky. Place in an oiled bowl and cover with plastic wrap. Refrigerate several hours or overnight. Turn dough onto generously floured surface. Pat dough to $^1/_2$-inch thickness. Cut with a 2-inch round cutter. Place on ungreased cookie sheet about 1 inch apart. Brush generously with melted butter. Allow rolls to rise at room temperature about 45 minutes to 1 hour. Bake in a preheated 400 degree oven for 10 minutes. Makes 24 rolls.

Cynthia Pedregon
Peach Tree Tea Room
Fredericksburg, Texas

Friends are like fancy chocolates—
it's what's inside that counts.

NOTES:

JUST DESSERTS

Candy by the pound, as well as delicious home-made fudge in many flavors, take you back to that old fashioned hometown feeling. A kid can buy a quarter's worth of candy here at the Gruene General Store, and a special feature is the toy area, where an emphasis is placed on old-fashioned toys such as jump ropes, jacks, marbles, and other nostalgic playthings.

Every square inch of the Gruene General Store is covered with collectible signs, returning you to times gone by and the days of your youth. For the nostalgia lover, the antique signs, many of which are hand-painted on wood, are a real treat. The antique fixtures, some advertising now-defunct brands, display more modern products or reproduction merchandise.

APPLE PIE

7 to 8 apples, sliced
Juice of ¹/₂ lemon
¹/₂ cup Aspen Mulling Spice
¹/₂ cup brown sugar (less if apples are sweet)
¹/₄ cup butter cut up and dotted in the apples
I tablespoon flour (a little more if the apples are juicy)

Mix all ingredients and place in a regular double pie crust recipe.
Flute top crust. Bake at 400 degrees for 10 minutes; then reduce to
350 degrees for 30 minutes.

ASPEN MULLING SPICE CO.
ASPEN, COLORADO

BUTTERMILK PECAN PIE

¹/₂ cup butter
2 cups sugar
2 teaspoons vanilla
3 eggs
3 tablespoons flour
¹/₄ teaspoon salt
I cup buttermilk
I (9-inch) unbaked pie shell
¹/₂ cup chopped pecans

Preheat oven to 300 degrees. Cream butter and sugar until light and
fluffy, adding ¹/₂ cup sugar at a time. Blend in vanilla. Add eggs, one
at a time. Combine flour and salt; add small amount at a time. Add
buttermilk. Sprinkle pecans in bottom of pie crust; pour custard mix
over the pecans and bake 1 hour 30 minutes at 300 degrees. The top
browns as it cooks. Best served at room temperature.

BUTTERSCOTCH BROWNIE PIE

4 egg whites
Pinch of salt
I cup sugar
I cup graham cracker crumbs
I teaspoon vanilla
¹/₂ cup chopped walnuts
Cool Whip or whipped cream (optional)

Beat egg whites with salt. Add sugar and beat until stiff peaks form. Fold in graham cracker crumbs, vanilla and nuts. Spoon into greased pie plate. Bake 325 degrees for 35 to 40 minutes. Cool, frost with Cool Whip or whipped cream, and refrigerate.

SHARI SHANNON
HUNTER JUNCTION
GRUENE TEXAS

ORANGE ANGEL PIE

Crust:
4 egg whites
$^1/_2$ teaspoon cream of tartar
$^3/_4$ cup sifted sugar

Filling:
1 or 1 $^1/_2$ cups whipping cream
2 or 3 tablespoons powdered sugar
4 or 6 egg yolks
$^1/_2$ to $^3/_4$ cup sugar
Pinch of salt
2 to 3 tablespoons orange juice
1 to 2 tablespoons lemon juice
1 teaspoon orange rind
1 teaspoon lemon rind

TOP:
$^1/_2$ pint whipping cream
4 tablespoons sugar

Crust: Beat egg whites until frothy, add cream of tartar and blend. Gradually add sugar, beating until stiff. Put in ungreased 9-inch pie pan and bake for 1 hour at 300 degrees. Cool.

Filling: Beat egg yolks, add sugar and rest of ingredients. Cook in double-boiler until thick. Cool. Whip cream with 2 to 3 tablespoons powdered sugar. Mix whipped cream with cooled pie filling and pour mixture into the meringue pie shell.

Top: Mix $^1/_2$ cup whipping cream with 4 tablespoons sugar. Whip and cover pie.

KYLE AND ETHELENE GRUENE
GRUENE TEXAS

PECAN-PUMPKIN PIE

*This is a different version of the standard pumpkin
pie. The pecans add a nice crunch.*

Pumpkin Layer:
1 egg
1 cup solid pack pumpkin
¹/₃ cup granulated sugar
1 teaspoon pumpkin spice mix

Pecan Layer:
2 eggs
²/₃ cup light corn syrup
¹/₂ cup granulated sugar
3 tablespoons butter, melted
¹/₂ teaspoon vanilla extract
1 cup pecan meats
1 unbaked deep dish pastry shell

Pumpkin layer: In medium bowl, beat egg. Stir in pumpkin, sugar
and pumpkin pie spice. Spread over bottom of pie shell.

Pecan layer: In same bowl, beat 2 eggs. Stir in corn syrup, sugar,
butter and vanilla. Stir in nuts. Spoon over pumpkin mixture. Bake
in preheated 350 degree oven for 50 minutes or until filling is set.
Cool on wire rack.

DAPHNE HUGHES

★

It's always something.
—Roseanne Roseannadanna
(Gilda Radner)

CRUNCHY-NUT MINCEMEAT PIE

This recipe comes from Barbara Richardson in Longview, Texas.
Pat says her family expects this pie each Christmas and Thanksgiving.

1 package mincemeat
1 ¹/₂ cups water
³/₄ cup sugar
1 cup plus 2 tablespoons flour
¹/₃ cup brown sugar
¹/₃ cup coconut
1 apple, chopped
1 cup chopped pecans
¹/₄ cup Mogen David wine
¹/₂ cup raisins
1 stick margarine
Unbaked pie crusts (2 small or 1 large)

Mix mincemeat, water, sugar and 2 tablespoons flour in saucepan and cook over medium heat until mixture begins to thicken. Remove from heat and pour into unbaked crusts (either 1 large or 2 small). Mix 1 cup flour and all remaining ingredients (brown sugar, coconut, apple, pecans, wine, raisins and margarine) until crumbly and sprinkle over mincemeat filling. Bake for about 40 minutes or until topping is golden brown.

PAT FRASE

TANTIE'S LEMON MERINGUE PIE

*My grandmother, Frances Harper Keys (Tantie to all her grandchildren)
was a fabulous and legendary cook. She always made this lemon
meringue pie for me, her chocolate pie for my brother, George, and
her pecan pie for my brother, Bob. That was a labor of love!*

5 tablespoons cornstarch
2 cups water
I cup sugar
¹/₄ teaspoon salt
2 egg yolks, slightly beaten
2 tablespoons butter
5 tablespoons lemon juice
2 teaspoons grated lemon rind
I large baked pie shell

Meringue:
2 egg whites
4 tablespoons sugar

In saucepan over medium heat, mix cornstarch with ¹/₂ cup cold
water, blend in sugar and salt. Add remainder of water, stir constantly until thick. Pour hot mixture over beaten egg yolks, stirring
constantly. Remove from heat, add butter, lemon juice and rind. Mix
well. Cool. Pour in baked pie shell.

Meringue: Beat egg whites until very stiff, gradually adding 4 tablespoons sugar. Pile on top of pie. Bake in slow oven (325 degrees) for
15 minutes. Cool and eat.

Texas ain't no place for amateurs.

TANTIE'S CHOCOLATE PIE

This was my brother George's favorite pie.

1 cup sugar
1 cup milk
heaping tablespoon flour
1 ½ tablespoons cocoa
2 tablespoons butter
2 beaten egg yolks
1 teaspoon vanilla
1 baked pie crust

Meringue:
2 egg whites
2 tablespoons sugar
½ teaspoon vanilla

In saucepan, mix sugar, flour and cocoa together. Add milk and butter and cook until thick, stirring constantly. Pour hot mixture over beaten egg yolks, stirring constantly. Add vanilla. Cool and pour into baked pie crust.

Meringue: Beat egg whites stiff, adding sugar gradually until peaks form. Add vanilla. Pile on top of pie and bake at 325 degrees for 15 minutes.

HELPFUL HINT:

Chocolate will stop the burning sensation in your mouth and help to soothe your stomach when you've eaten too much spicy food.

TANTIE'S PECAN PIE

This was the pie Tantie made especially for my brother, Bob.

1 **cup sugar**
3 **eggs**
1 **cup corn syrup**
1 **tablespoon flour**
1 **tablespoon butter, melted**
1 **cup pecan halves**
1 **unbaked pie crust**

Beat 3 eggs, adding sugar gradually, with flour and melted butter. Add syrup, stirring to mix well. Add pecans, stirring to coat. Pour into unbaked pie crust. Bake at 450 degrees for 10 minutes. Reduce oven to 350 degrees and bake for 40 minutes or until center is firm.

BOB AND MARILYN KEYS

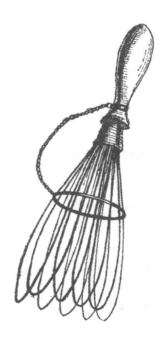

VELVETY CUSTARD PIE

Unbelievable! This 1920's pie bakes in just 15 minutes!

4 eggs, slightly beaten
¹/₂ cup sugar
¹/₄ teaspoon salt
I teaspoon vanilla
2 ¹/₂ cups milk, scalded
I (9-inch) unbaked pie shell
Nutmeg

Thoroughly mix eggs, sugar, salt and vanilla. Slowly stir in hot milk. At once, pour into unbaked pastry shell. Dash top with nutmeg. Bake at 475 degrees for 5 minutes; reduce heat to 425 degrees and bake 10 minutes longer (or until knife inserted halfway between center and edge comes out clean). Cool on rack. Serve cool, or chill.

THE TIMMERMANN SISTERS
GERONIMO, TEXAS

★

GERMAN SWEET CHOCOLATE PIE

I (4 ounce) package German Sweet Chocolate
¹/₄ cup butter
I (14.5 ounce) can evaporated milk
I ¹/₂ cups sugar
3 tablespoons cornstarch
¹/₈ teaspoon salt
2 eggs
I teaspoon vanilla
I unbaked 10-inch deep dish pie shell, or
2 unbaked 8-inch pie shells
I ¹/₃ cups sweetened, flaked coconut
¹/₂ cup chopped pecans

Melt chocolate with butter over low heat, stirring until blended. Remove from heat; gradually blend in evaporated milk. Mix sugar, cornstarch, and salt thoroughly. Beat in eggs and vanilla. Gradually blend in chocolate mixture. Pour into pie shell(s). Combine coconut and nuts, sprinkle over filling. Bake at 375 degrees for 45 minutes. Filling will be soft, but will set while cooling. Cool at least 4 hours before cutting.

THE TIMMERMANN SISTERS
GERONIMO, TEXAS

★

PECAN TARTS

Crust:
1 (3 ounce) package cream cheese
$^1/_2$ cup margarine or butter
1 cup flour

Filling:
1 egg
$^3/_4$ cup brown sugar
1 tablespoon margarine
1 teaspoon vanilla
Dash of salt
1 cup pecan pieces

Preheat oven to 325 degrees.

Crust: Soften cream cheese and butter; blend. Stir in flour. Chill about 1 hour. Shape into 1-inch balls. Place in TINY ungreased muffin cups. Press dough on bottom and sides.

Filling: Beat together until smooth all except pecans. Chop pecans coarsely and sprinkle in each of the pastry-lined cups. Add filling by using a teaspoon. Bake 30 minutes. Cool. Remove from pans.

DAPHNE HUGHES

CHRISTMAS STOLLEN

A wonderful gift from the kitchen for friends and neighbors.
The Timmermann sisters give this fruit bread a top rating.

1 cup milk
1 cup butter or margarine, melted
1/2 cup water
5 1/4 cups flour
1/4 cup sugar
1 teaspoon salt
2 packages active dry yeast
2 eggs, beaten
1/2 teaspoon grated lemon rind
1/2 teaspoon grated orange rind
1/2 cup seedless raisins
1/2 cup candied fruit, chopped
1/2 cup nuts, chopped
3 tablespoons butter or margarine, softened
1/2 cup sugar
1 tablespoon ground cinnamon

Combine milk, 1 cup melted butter and 1/2 cup water in a small sauce-pan; place over low heat just until lukewarm. Combine flour, 1/4 cup sugar, salt and yeast in a large mixing bowl; stir in warm milk mixture and eggs, mixing well. Add lemon and orange rind, raisins, fruit and nuts; mix well. Cover dough and refrigerate overnight.

Place chilled dough on a lightly floured surface; roll into an 18x12-inch rectangle; spread with 3 tablespoons soft butter. Combine 1/2 cup sugar and cinnamon; sprinkle over butter. Beginning with long edge, roll up dough jellyroll fashion, pinching edges to seal. If ends are smaller than remainder of roll, trim off (about 1 inch). Place roll on a large greased cookie sheet, and shape into a ring (it should resemble a large doughnut). Brush ends of roll with water, and pinch together to seal. Using kitchen shears, make cuts in dough every inch around ring, cutting two-thirds of the way through roll at each cut. Gently turn each piece of dough on its side, slightly overlapping the previous piece.

Let rise in a warm place, uncovered, 1 hour. Bake at 350 degrees for 25 to 30 minutes or until golden brown. Drizzle glaze over hot ring. Decorate with candied cherry halves.

GLAZE

1 cup powdered sugar
2 to 3 tablespoons water or milk
¼ teaspoon vanilla extract
Candied cherry halves for decoration

Combine powdered sugar, water and vanilla until smooth.

THE TIMMERMANN SISTERS
GERONIMO, TEXAS

★

MAMA'S BAKED APPLES

My grandmother, Lena Mistrot, used to make this for dessert when I was a child. Back then, she used a conventional oven, which can still be done, but I find a microwave bakes these apples perfectly. This is a good, quick, healthy dessert that is very satisfying. The red hots turn the apples a nice rosy color.

Apples, any kind, red or green
Red hot candies

Core apples and fill cavities with red hots. Place in a casserole or pie plate and pour about 1-inch of water in bottom of dish. Cover with plastic wrap. Microwave on high for 2 minutes; rotate dish and microwave again for 2 minutes; continue this process, depending on the amount of apples being prepared, allowing 2 minutes per apple. When apples feel soft to the touch, remove from microwave and allow to rest for 30 minutes still covered. Serve with milk or ice cream, if desired.

QUICK COBBLER

Anne says she got this quick and easy dessert recipe from her Aunt Mickey.

¹/₄ pound butter or margarine (1 stick)
1 cup sugar
1 cup flour
1 ¹/₂ teaspoons baking powder
³/₄ cup milk
2 cups fruit, any kind, fresh or canned (drained)

Melt butter in oblong baking dish. Mix flour, sugar, baking powder and milk together and pour over butter in baking dish. Do not stir. Arrange fruit on top to cover butter. Sprinkle additional sugar over fruit according to sweetness desired (¹/₂ cup). Bake 30 to 40 minutes at 375 degrees.

ANNE McGILVRAY

QUICK & EASY COBBLER

This is fast and easy, and really good!

1 stick butter or margarine
1 cup flour
1 cup sugar
1 cup milk
1 can fruit pie filling, any flavor

Preheat oven to 350 degrees. In 13x9-inch pan, melt butter in oven. Remove from oven and pour pie filling over butter. In medium bowl, combine flour, sugar and milk and pour over fruit filling. Swirl with knife. Bake for approximately 30 minutes.

BETH CROCKER

APPLE STRUDEL COBBLER

1 (21 ounce) can apple pie filling or
   Fresh sliced apples, slightly cooked in small amount of
   water and sugar
1 cup coconut
1 cup broken pecan pieces
$^1/_2$ cup cherries, halved
$^1/_4$ cup brown sugar
$^1/_2$ cup Bisquick mix
1 tablespoon sugar
$^1/_4$ teaspoon cinnamon
Dash of nutmeg
3 tablespoons buttermilk

Heat pie filling (or fresh apples), coconut, pecans, cherries and brown sugar to boiling over medium heat. Put into greased 8x8-inch or 7x11-inch pan. Mix Bisquick mix, sugar, cinnamon, nutmeg and buttermilk together. Drop by spoonful over apple mixture and sprinkle with sugar and cinnamon. Bake in 325 to 350 degree oven until golden brown. Can be served warm, with ice cream.

ELENORA KOHLENBERG

HELPFUL HINT:

Fill your coffeepot with white vinegar
and run it through several cycles
to clean it; then run through
a cycle with plain water to rinse.

FRUIT CRISP

This recipe came from Beth's mother-in-law,
Bobbie Crocker. It was a family favorite!

1 box white or yellow cake mix
2 sticks butter or margarine
1 can fruit pie filling (apple or cherry is best)
Cool Whip or ice cream (optional)

Preheat oven to 350 degrees. Melt 1 stick of margarine in 13x9-inch pan. Pour pie filling over butter. Cover filling with cake mix (dry). Cut second stick of butter into thin pats and place over cake mix (try to cover entire pan). Bake for 25 to 30 minutes. Serve with Cool Whip or scoop of ice cream.

BETH CROCKER

★

BARBARA BUSH'S APPLE CRISP

My friend, Fran Strasser, gave me this recipe. It's so good!

4 cups sliced, peeled apples
¹/₄ cup orange juice
¹/₂ cup sugar
³/₄ cup flour
¹/₂ teaspoon cinnamon
¹/₄ teaspoon nutmeg
Dash salt
¹/₃ cup butter

Butter pie plate. Place apples in pan and pour orange juice over them. Combine sugar, flour and spices and cut in butter. Sprinkle over apples. Bake at 375 degrees for 45 minutes.

TRIED AND PROVEN PEACH CRISP RECIPE

The boiling water creates a crisp, shiny topping that is really different.

3 cups sliced fresh peaches
¹/₄ cup butter, softened
1 ³/₄ cups sugar, divided
1 teaspoon baking powder
1 cup all-purpose flour
¹/₂ cup milk
¹/₂ teaspoon salt
¹/₄ teaspoon ground nutmeg
1 tablespoon cornstarch
1 cup boiling water
Whipping cream or ice cream (optional)

Place peach slices in an 8-inch square baking pan. Cream butter and ³/₄ cup sugar. Combine flour, baking powder and salt; add to creamed mixture alternately with milk. Spoon mixture over fruit. Sift together 1 cup sugar, cornstarch and nutmeg; sprinkle over batter. Pour boiling water over top. Bake at 350 degrees for 1 hour. Serve with whipping cream or ice cream, if desired. Yield: 6 servings.

FRAN STRASSER

There's no place like home.

RICE PUDDING

*This is the ultimate comfort food. Good for
what ails you, or even if nothing does.*

2 cups cooked rice
¹/₃ cup sugar
2 eggs
¹/₂ cup raisins
Juice and rind of 1 orange
Juice and rind of 1/2 lemon
¹/₄ teaspoon salt

Soak raisins in juices for 30 minutes to 1 hour. Beat sugar and eggs, add rest of ingredients and bake in buttered casserole at 350 degrees for 40 minutes.

★

BANANDY FREEZE

*This is a simple, yet elegant, party dessert. I call it my "easy
Bananas Foster recipe." All ingredients except the ice cream
can be prepared ahead; then at dessert time, just blend in ice cream,
pour into chilled glasses and serve. Be sure to place the empty serving
dishes in the freezer to chill before filling with the dessert.*

1 quart good real French vanilla ice cream
1 banana
¹/₂ cup banana liqueur
¹/₂ cup brandy

Blend all ingredients in blender. Pour into sherbert or widemouthed champagne glasses and sip almost frozen. Serves 6 to 8.

FREEZER FRUIT SHERBERT

Good, and good for you!

4 medium bananas
I (20 ounce) can crushed pineapple, undrained
I (16 ounce) bottle maraschino cherries,
   undrained (remove stems)
I (6 ounce) can frozen orange juice concentrate, undiluted
I cup milk
¹/₄ cup lemon juice
¹/₂ cup sugar

Combine first 3 ingredients in container of an electric blender; blend until smooth. Pour mixture into large mixing bowl. Combine remaining ingredients in container of electric blender. Blend until smooth, and then add to blended fruit. Mix all ingredients well; cover and freeze until firm. Yield: about 2 quarts.

EASY POTS DE CREME

This is very rich, so a small serving is a perfect dessert.

I (6 ounce) package semi-sweet chocolate chips
¹/₂ (I I ¹/₂ ounces) package milk chocolate chips
¹/₂ cup sugar
3 eggs
I cup hot milk
¹/₂ teaspoon almond extract

In blender combine chips, sugar and eggs while motor is running. Pour in hot milk and blend on medium speed until smooth. Pour into sherbert glasses or demitasse cups and chill several hours. May be garnished with whipped cream or orange slices. Makes 8.

COFFEE BAVARIAN

Prepare this in a springform pan for a special occasion.

1 cup fine graham cracker crumbs
¹/₄ cup melted butter or margarine
1 envelope unflavored gelatin
¹/₂ cup cold water
¹/₂ cup sugar
1 tablespoon instant coffee
¹/₄ teaspoon salt
1 ²/₃ cups evaporated milk
1 cup shaved chocolate

Mix cracker crumbs and melted butter. Line bottom of 8-inch square pan with mixture and chill. In 1 quart saucepan, soften gelatin in cold water. Add sugar, coffee and salt. Stir over low heat until sugar and gelatin dissolve. Remove from heat. Stir in 1 cup of the evaporated milk. Pour into small bowl of electric mixer and chill until firm. Then beat at low speed until mixture is just broken up. Add ²/₃ cup evaporated milk. Beat at high speed until mixture fills bowl, then pour it over crumbs in pan. Sprinkle shaved chocolate over top and chill until firm. To serve, cut into squares. This may be prepared several days ahead.

ELEGANT ORANGES

This is so good and easy, and impresses everyone because it is really a beautiful dessert. A good chocolate cookie on the side of the dessert plate is a nice touch and compliments the tartness of the sherbert.

Large perfect oranges, one for each person
Pineapple or orange sherbert
Mint leaves or chocolate curls to garnish

With a sharp knife, cut the top off each orange and hollow out with a grapefruit spoon. Save the orange pulp for another use. Cut a thin slice off the bottom if necessary to stand upright. Turn upside down to drain. Soften the sherbert enough so that it is easy to scoop, and fill the orange cups with the sherbert, mounding slightly on top. Place on waxed paper on cookie sheet and place in freezer. Remove from freezer 15 minutes before serving to soften slightly. Garnish with mint or a chocolate curl.

CHERRY DESSERT

This is pretty, as well as delicious.

I Angel Food Cake
I medium carton Cool Whip
I (8 ounce) container sour cream
I package vanilla instant pudding
I can cherry pie filling

Tear angel food cake into bite-sized pieces and set aside. Prepare pudding according to directions on package. Mix cake, Cool Whip, sour cream and pudding. Put in a large dessert bowl and top with pie filling.

TAMMY HUNTER

ANGEL PIES

*I have impressed many a dinner guest with this dessert. It is
easy, can be made ahead (I have even successfully frozen
the meringue shells) and is tart and delicious.*

Meringue Shells:
Dash of salt
¹/₂ teaspoon vinegar
¹/₄ teaspoon vanilla
3 egg whites
1 cup sugar

Lemon Sauce:
¹/₂ cup butter
4 eggs
1 ¹/₂ cups sugar
¹/₂ cup plus 2 tablespoons lemon juice
1 tablespoon cornstarch
1 tablespoon lemon peel, grated

To make the meringue shells: Add salt, vinegar and vanilla to egg
whites; beat until mixture forms peaks. Add sugar gradually, beating after each addition and beating until stiff peaks form. Spoon
into 6 large mounds on a cookie sheet lined with plain ungreased
paper (I use a brown paper sack). Shape into cups with the back of a
spoon. Bake at 300 degrees for 45 minutes. Remove from paper immediately to a rack and cool thoroughly.

To make the sauce: Melt butter on low heat. In a food processor,
blend eggs, sugar, lemon juice and cornstarch. Add to the melted
butter and cook slowly on low heat, stirring constantly, until thick.
This takes 8 to 10 minutes. Remove from heat and add lemon peel.
Cool.

At serving time, fill the hollows of the meringues with the sauce. Garnish with a twist of lemon peel, a sprig of fresh mint, or a dollop of whipped topping.

If there's any lemon sauce left over, it is wonderful over angel food cake. The lemon sauce will keep in the refrigerator for a week or so.

BANANA PUDDING

Made-from-scratch vanilla pudding makes this old-fashioned dessert something out of the ordinary. It is so much better than the boxed pudding and not at all hard to make.

¹/₃ cup sugar
¹/₄ cup cornstarch
¹/₈ teaspoon salt
2 ³/₄ cups milk
2 tablespoons butter
I teaspoon vanilla
3 or 4 bananas
¹/₂ box vanilla wafers

In a saucepan, combine sugar, cornstarch and salt. Gradually stir in milk until smooth. Stirring constantly, bring to a boil over medium heat and cook 1 minute until thickened. Remove from heat and stir in vanilla and butter. Cool slightly. Line the bottom of a dish with vanilla wafers and then stand a row of vanilla wafers on their sides around the edge of the dish. Put a layer of the pudding, then a layer of sliced bananas, repeating the layers and extending another row of vanilla wafers around the edge of the dish if necessary, finishing with a layer of pudding. Crush about 10 of the wafers in a plastic bag and sprinkle them on the top of the dish. Serve at room temperature for best flavor, but refrigerate leftovers.

CHUCKWAGON CHOCOLATE BONANZA

1 pound semi-sweet Baker's chocolate
1 ¼ pounds butter
6 whole eggs
5 cups sugar
1 tablespoon vanilla
2 ¾ cups cake flour
⅔ cup cocoa powder
1 pound chopped pecans
Vanilla ice cream
Chocolate syrup
Maraschino cherries

Melt the chocolate and butter in a microwave. In a separate container, mix the eggs, sugar and vanilla with a wire whisk until the mixture appears glossy. Add the melted chocolate and butter to the egg mixture and mix well with a wire whisk. Sift the cake flour and cocoa powder together in a separate bowl. Gently fold the flour and cocoa and all of the pecans into the chocolate and egg mixture. Line a 12x18x2-inch baking pan with parchment paper and grease the paper and the insides of the pan. Transfer the brownie mixture into the pan and bake uncovered at 350 degrees for 40 minutes. Serve warm, topped with vanilla ice cream, chocolate syrup and a maraschino cherry.

SALTGRASS STEAKHOUSE
HOUSTON, DALLAS AND
SAN ANTONIO, TEXAS

I'd stop eating chocolate, but I'm no quitter!

CHOCOLATE DELIGHT

This recipe comes from Tammy's mom, and has been a family favorite for years.

1 cup flour
1 stick butter
¹/₂ cup chopped pecans
1 (8 ounce) package cream cheese, softened
1 cup powdered sugar
2 small packages chocolate instant pudding
3 cups milk
1 cup Cool Whip
1 chocolate bar, grated

Mix flour, butter and pecans. Place in 9x13-inch Pyrex pan and bake 15 minutes at 375 degrees for crust. Mix cream cheese, powdered sugar, and Cool Whip together and spread on crust. Mix pudding and milk together and spread on top of cream cheese mixture. Top with Cool Whip and grated chocolate bar.

TAMMY HUNTER

MARILYN'S MAGNIFICENT CHOCOLATE MEDALLION CAKE

*This cake is definitely worth making, baking and eating.
It is the benchmark for all chocolate cakes!*

¹/₄ **cup butter**

¹/₄ **cup shortening**

2 **cups sugar**

2 **eggs, unbeaten**

2 **cups sifted cake flour (minus 2 tablespoons if not cake flour)**

¹/₈ **teaspoon salt**

³/₄ **cup cocoa**

³/₄ **cup boiling water**

1 ¹/₂ **teaspoons baking soda**

1 **cup buttermilk**

1 **teaspoon vanilla**

Preheat oven to 350 degrees. Grease and flour two 9-inch cake pans; set aside. Cream butter and shortening together; add sugar gradually, creaming until light and fluffy. Add eggs, one at a time, beating well. Sift flour and salt together in medium bowl; set aside. In a heatproof bowl, make a smooth paste of cocoa and boiling water; cool slightly. In a medium bowl, stir baking soda into buttermilk. Add flour mixture to creamed mixture, alternating with buttermilk and soda, beginning and ending with flour mixture. Blend cocoa and water thoroughly. Add vanilla and blend into batter. Mix batter well and pour into prepared pans. Bake 35 minutes at 350 degrees. Cake is done when center springs back after light touch. Cool 10 minutes. Remove from pans. Cool thoroughly and frost.

COCOA MEDALLION FROSTING

³/₄ **cup cocoa**

4 **cups powdered sugar, sifted**

¹/₂ **cup butter**

1 **teaspoon vanilla**

¹/₂ **cup evaporated milk**

Mix cocoa and sugar. Cream part of cocoa with butter. Blend in the vanilla and half the milk. Add remaining cocoa and sugar mixture, blending well. Add remaining milk and beat to desired spreading consistency (additional milk may be added if needed).

BOB AND MARILYN KEYS

SALAD DRESSING CAKE

1 ¹/₂ **cups salad dressing or mayonnaise**
1 ¹/₂ **cups sugar**
6 **tablespoons cocoa**
3 **teaspoons baking soda**
3 **cups sifted flour**
1 ¹/₂ **teaspoon vanilla**
1 ¹/₂ **cups water**

Mix in order given. Bake 60 minutes in a greased and floured bundt pan or 30 minutes in an oblong pan at 350 degrees until done. Frost when cool with Buttercream Frosting.

BUTTERCREAM FROSTING
1 **stick butter, softened**
1 **box powdered sugar**
Dash of salt
¹/₂ **teaspoon vanilla**
Milk

Beat together, adding milk to desired consistency.

MELANIE QUINN

CHRISTMAS DATE CAKE

This cake is traditional at holidays in the Gruene family.

1 pound dates
1 pound pecans
¹/₂ pound glacéed cherries
¹/₂ pound glacéed pineapple
1 cup sugar
4 eggs
1 cup all-purpose flour, divided
2 teaspoons baking powder
¹/₂ teaspoon salt
1 teaspoon vanilla
3 small loaf pans, 4x8-inch, lined with wax paper

In a mixing bowl, cut up dates, cherries and pineapple. Add the pecans and 1 ¹/₂ tablespoons of flour and mix. In another bowl, make batter (sugar, eggs, flour, baking powder, salt and vanilla). Pour batter over fruit and nuts, mixing well. Pour mixture into wax paper lined pans. Bake 1 ¹/₂ hours at 300 degrees. To add decoration, place 6 pecan halves on top of each cake before baking.

KYLE AND ETHELENE GRUENE
GRUENE TEXAS

If you want to be happy for an hour,
drink wine;
If you want to be happy for a day, run away;
If you want to be happy for a year,
get married;
If you want to be happy forever,
be a gardener.

MARY LOUISE BARRY'S APPLESAUCE CAKE

Elizabeth's mother-in-law always makes this cake for holidays.

2 ¹/₂ cups hot applesauce, homemade (recipe follows)
3 teaspoons baking soda
I cup Crisco
2 cups sugar
I cup pecans, chopped
I cup dates (pitted and sliced)
I cup prunes (stewed)
I teaspoon nutmeg
¹/₂ teaspoon cloves
4 cups flour
I tablespoon cocoa

To make the homemade applesauce, stew about four sliced or chopped cooking apples in one cup of water until soft. Mash slightly. Add soda to hot applesauce. This is very important.

Cream in large bowl the sugar and Crisco. Sift flour and cocoa with nutmeg and cloves. Add alternately the dry ingredients and hot applesauce to the sugar-Crisco mixture. Add nuts and fruit. Use one tube pan, greased and floured. Bake at 300 degrees for 2¹/₂- 3 hours. Wrap cake in foil while still hot.

ELIZABETH BARRY

BLITZ KUCHEN
(Lightning Cake)

This quick and easy cake was a favorite of Cindy's great-grandmother, Emma Schaefer Voigt, and was baked often in a stone oven outdoors.

2 cups flour
3 teaspoons baking powder
¹/₂ cup butter or margarine (I stick)
I cup sugar
2 eggs
I teaspoon vanilla
³/₄ cup hot milk

Cream butter, sugar and eggs. Add vanilla. Combine flour and baking powder. Add dry ingredients to mixture, alternating with hot milk. Put in greased baking pan and sprinkle top with sugar and cinnamon before baking. Bake at 350 degrees, 20 to 30 minutes.

CYNTHIA HARTMANN NEALEIGH

BLITZ KUCHEN TOO
(Lightning Cake)

I don't know why it was called this ("Lightning Cake") except it's fast like "lightning" to make!

¹/₂ pound butter (no substitute)
I cup sugar
5 eggs
I ¹/₂ cups flour
2 teaspoons baking powder
Pinch of salt

Cream sugar and butter. Beat, adding eggs one at a time. Add dry ingredients which have been sifted together. Pour in shallow (12x16-inch) pan. Sprinkle with sugar and cinnamon and bake at 350 degrees until done.

Eleanor Coldeway

KAHLUA CAKE

1 box Devil's Food cake mix
1 cup Kahlua (use as a substitute for 1 cup water)
¹/₃ cup water
¹/₂ cup oil
3 eggs
¹/₂ to 1 package semi-sweet mini-morsels

Icing:
¹/₂ cup whipping cream
6 ounces cream cheese
¹/₄ pound butter
1 teaspoon vanilla
1 box powdered sugar

Cake: Follow mixing instructions on cake mix box, substituting 1 cup Kahlua for 1 cup water. Fold mini-morsels into mix before baking. Follow baking instructions on box.

Icing: Mix whipping cream, cream cheese and butter together and let come to room temperature. Mix powdered sugar and vanilla into ROOM TEMPERATURE whipping cream mixture; beat until thick and smooth. Apply to cool cake.

Bill Cone

APRICOT SAVANNAH CAKE

*Anyone who has ever eaten at the Peach Tree Tea Room
knows what delicious food is served there. This cake is definitely
worth the effort — it tastes and looks divine.*

1 cup dried apricots, chopped coarsely
¹/₂ cup dry sherry
³/₄ cup butter, room temperature
¹/₄ cup brown sugar
³/₄ cup white sugar
3 eggs
1 ¹/₂ teaspoons vanilla
Zest of 1 orange
2 ¹/₂ cups flour
1 ¹/₂ teaspoons baking soda
¹/₂ teaspoon salt
1 ¹/₂ cups buttermilk
¹/₂ cup toasted walnuts, chopped
1 cup semi-sweet chocolate chips, chopped coarsely

Soak apricots in sherry for several hours or overnight. Preheat oven
to 350 degrees. Using an electric mixer, cream the butter and the
sugars together in a large bowl. Add the eggs, one at a time, beating
well after each addition. Beat in the vanilla and the orange zest.
Combine the flour, baking soda and salt. Add alternately with the
buttermilk, beating well after each addition. Stir in the apricots with
the sherry, walnuts and chocolate chips. Pour the batter into 3 greased
and floured 9-inch round cake pans. Bake for 35 to 40 minutes or
until toothpick inserted in center comes out clean. Cool cakes in
pans for 10 minutes. Invert on wire racks and cool slightly. Spread
the Chocolate Ganache between the layers while the cake is still
warm. Use the Cream Cheese Frosting to frost the sides and top of
the cake. Press the walnuts onto the lower half on side of cake.

CHOCOLATE GANACHE

1 ¹/₂ cups semi-sweet chocolate chips
1 cup heavy whipping cream

Melt the chocolate slowly. Pour the melted chocolate into a mixing bowl. Using a whisk, pour the whipping cream slowly into the chocolate. Continue to mix until smooth. Spread the ganache between the cake layers while the cake and the ganache are still warm.

CREAM CHEESE FROSTING

¹/₄ cup butter, room temperature
8 ounces cream cheese, room temperature
1 pound powdered sugar
2 tablespoons orange liqueur
2 tablespoons orange zest

Using an electric mixer, cream the butter and cream cheese. Add the powdered sugar and orange liqueur. Beat until smooth and add the zest. This frosts three layers and sides of cake.

CYNTHIA PEDREGON
PEACH TREE TEA ROOM
FREDERICKSBURG, TEXAS

Life is uncertain--
eat dessert first.

OATMEAL CAKE

1 cup oatmeal

1 1/2 cups boiling water

1 cup sugar

1 cup brown sugar

2 sticks butter or margarine

1 1/2 cups flour

2 eggs

1 teaspoon baking soda

2 teaspoons cinnamon

1 teaspoon nutmeg

Pour boiling water over oatmeal and let cool. Cream together the sugars and butter. Add the flour, eggs, baking soda, cinnamon and nutmeg. Add oatmeal. Bake in loaf pan at 350 degrees approximately 45 to 60 minutes. Top with German Chocolate Icing.

GERMAN CHOCOLATE ICING

1 cup evaporated milk

1 cup sugar

3 egg yolks

1/2 cup butter or margarine

1 teaspoon vanilla

1 1/3 cups coconut

1 cup chopped pecans

Combine milk, sugar, egg yolks, butter and vanilla in saucepan. Cook over medium heat, stirring constantly until mixture thickens, about 12 minutes. Remove from heat. Add coconut and pecans. Cool until of spreading consistency, beating occasionally. Makes 2 1/2 cups.

CHOCOLATE SHEET CAKE

I got this recipe years ago from Clara Mae Dickerson. My family usually requests it for birthdays. Using the same saucepan for the cake and the frosting makes it an easy cleanup. It's best made a day ahead so that the flavors can "marry".

2 cups all-purpose flour
2 cups sugar
2 sticks butter or margarine
3 $1/2$ heaping tablespoons cocoa
I cup water
2 eggs
$1/2$ cup buttermilk mixed with I teaspoon baking soda
I teaspoon vanilla

Preheat oven to 350 degrees. Grease and lightly flour sheet pan (11x13-inch). Mix flour and sugar. In a saucepan, bring margarine, cocoa and water to a boil. Pour over flour mixture. Mix and beat about 1 minute. Add eggs, buttermilk and vanilla. Beat 2 minutes. Pour into prepared pan and bake about 30 minutes. Frost with Chocolate Icing while cake is still hot.

CHOCOLATE ICING

I stick butter or margarine
3 $1/2$ tablespoons cocoa
$1/3$ cup milk
I pound powdered sugar
I teaspoon vanilla

As soon as cake is in the oven, in same saucepan used for cake, bring to a boil the margarine, cocoa and milk. Stir in sugar and vanilla. Beat until smooth. Spread on hot cake.

CHOCOLATE CHEESECAKE

Cheesecake can be made 2 to 3 days in advance and kept, covered with plastic wrap, in the refrigerator. Or, the cake can be frozen for up to 3 weeks. Defrost before serving.

Crust:
2 cups chocolate wafer crumbs
5 tablespoons butter, melted

Filling:
3 (8 ounce) packages cream cheese, at room temperature
1 cup sugar
5 large eggs
2 ounces (2 squares) semisweet chocolate, melted

Frosting:
6 ounces (6 squares) semisweet chocolate, melted
1/2 cup sour cream

Preheat oven to 300 degrees.

Crust: In a medium bowl, mix together chocolate crumbs and melted butter until well blended. Press into a 9-inch springform pan.

Filling: In a large bowl, beat together cream cheese, sugar and eggs at medium speed until smooth and fluffy. Spoon half of cream cheese mixture into crust. Stir chocolate into remaining cream cheese mixture until well blended. Drizzle over batter in crust to make swirls. Bake cheesecake for 50 minutes. Transfer pan to a wire rack. Cool completely. Transfer cheesecake to a serving plate, cover with plastic wrap, and chill for 2 hours. Uncover cheesecake; carefully remove the side of pan.

Frosting: In a small bowl, mix together chocolate and sour cream. Spread over cheesecake. Chill briefly until frosting is set.

TERRY ZENGLER

ICE BOX CHEESECAKE

Crust:
2 ¹/₂ **cups graham cracker crumbs**
1 **stick butter or margarine**
¹/₂ **cup sugar**

Filling:
1 **small package lemon Jello**
1 **cup boiling water**
1 **(8 ounce) package cream cheese**
3 **tablespoons lemon juice**
1 **can evaporated milk (chilled)**
³/₄ **cup sugar**

Crust: Melt butter, blend with sugar and graham cracker crumbs. Press ²/₃ of this mixture in bottom of 12x8-¹/₂-inch baking dish. Chill.

Filling: Dissolve Jello in hot water. Chill until it starts to thicken. Soften cream cheese and beat into Jello mixture. Beat chilled milk to whipped cream consistency. Gradually add sugar, cream cheese mixture and lemon juice. Pour over graham crackers. Sprinkle remaining crackers on top. Chill 4 hours.

PAT TEPE

My life will always have dirty dishes;
if this sink can become a place of
contemplation,
let me learn constancy here.
—Gunilla Norris

APPLE CHIP CAKE

This is almost like a spice cake, and is great for holiday gatherings.

1 cup white sugar
1 cup brown sugar
3 cups flour
1 teaspoon cinnamon
$^1/_2$ teaspoon salt
$^1/_2$ teaspoon baking soda
1 cup oil
2 eggs
2 teaspoons vanilla
1 cup chopped nuts
2 large apples, chipped (diced) with peeling

In large bowl, mix oil and sugars. Sift flour with salt, soda and cinnamon. Add eggs, flour mixture and spices and mix thoroughly. Fold in nuts and apples. Dough will be thick and sticky. Bake in greased and floured loaf or tube pan at 350 degrees for one hour.

TERRY ZENGLER

SAUERKRAUT CAKE

The sauerkraut makes this a very moist cake.

²/₃ cup butter or margarine
1 ¹/₂ cups sugar
3 eggs, beaten
1 cup water
¹/₂ cup cocoa
1 teaspoon baking soda
1 teaspoon baking powder
¹/₄ teaspoon salt
2 ¹/₄ cups flour, sifted
²/₃ cup drained, chopped sauerkraut
1 tablespoon vanilla

Cream butter and sugar, add beaten eggs, sauerkraut and vanilla. Sift dry ingredients and add alternately with 1 cup water. Pour into greased and floured 9x13-inch pan. Bake at 350 degrees for 30 minutes. Cool. Frost with cream cheese icing.

CREAM CHEESE ICING

1 stick margarine
1 (8 ounce) package cream cheese, softened
¹/₄ cup cocoa
2 ¹/₂ cups powdered sugar, sifted
1 teaspoon vanilla

Cream together the margarine and cream cheese. Add vanilla. Mix in cocoa and powdered sugar, beating until desired consistency.

ELENORA KOHLENBERG

MINNEHAHA KUCHEN

This is a very old recipe.

¹/₂ cup butter
1 ¹/₂ cups sugar
3 egg yolks
1 cup milk
2 ¹/₂ cups flour
2 teaspoons baking powder
1 teaspoon vanilla

Mix flour and baking powder together. Set aside. Beat butter and sugar together, adding egg yolks until creamy. Add vanilla and then add milk and flour mixture alternately. Bake in 3 (8-inch) layers in 350 degree oven.

FRUIT FILLING

1 tablespoon chopped citron
1 tablespoon raisins
¹/₂ pound almonds (without skins), or
     ¹/₂ pound pecans
¹/₂ pound chopped figs
3 egg whites, beaten
¹/₂ cup sugar

Beat egg whites with sugar. Stir in fruit and nuts. Spread fruit filling between each cake layer and frost with cream icing.

CREAM ICING

2 cups milk
2 eggs
3 tablespoons corn starch
1 cup sugar
1 teaspoon vanilla

Heat the milk in a double-boiler. Dissolve the cornstarch in a little cold milk and add to heated milk. Stir and cook over boiling water until smooth. Add sugar and cook 10 minutes. Add eggs and cook 4 minutes. Take off heat and add vanilla. Frost top and sides of cake.

ELEANOR COLDEWAY

COLORVISION CAKE

This recipe is from the 1950's and was served by Terry's mother, Lownie Oetken, every Sunday for dessert.

Cake:
1 package yellow cake mix
3 tablespoons any flavor Jello

Icing:
Remainder of Jello package
2 egg whites
1 cup sugar
$^1/_2$ teaspoon cream of tartar
$^1/_4$ cup water

Add 3 tablespoons Jello to cake mix and mix and bake according to package directions.

While cake is baking, prepare icing: Mix all ingredients in top of double-boiler. Over boiling water, beat with electric mixer until icing holds soft peaks. Remove from boiling water and beat until peaks stiffen. Cool and frost cake.

TERRY ZENGLER

Never trust a skinny cook.

CRUMB CAKE

³/₄ cup plus 2 tablespoons butter
1 cup sugar
1 egg
3 ¹/₃ cups flour
1 teaspoon baking powder
9 ounces Fischer & Wieser Apricot Preserves

In small bowl, blend flour and baking powder. Set aside. Beat butter and sugar with blender (low to medium speed) until creamy. Stir in egg. Add 1/2 of flour mixture. Blend until smooth. Remove bowl from blender and add remaining flour mixture. Blend by hand. Batter should be crumbly. Pour half of batter in bottom of lightly greased 9-inch cake pan. Pat down. Spread preserves over the layer of batter. Pour remaining batter on top of preserves. Do not pat down. Bake at 425 degrees until lightly browned, approximately 20 minutes. Sprinkle with powdered sugar to decorate. (Any flavor of jams or preserves may be substituted.)

FISCHER & WIESER SPECIALTY FOODS
FREDERICKSBURG, TEXAS

APPLE GOOD CAKE

3 eggs
1 cup oil
2 cups sugar
$^1/_2$ cup water
1 teaspoon cinnamon
$^1/_2$ teaspoon cloves
$^1/_2$ teaspoon nutmeg
$^1/_2$ teaspoon baking soda
1 teaspoon vanilla
$^1/_2$ teaspoon salt
3 cups flour
3 peeled apples
1 cup pecans

In a large bowl, thoroughly mix all ingredients except apples. Cut the apples into chunks, and add apples and pecans to the batter. If batter seems too thick, add a little more water. Bake at 325 degrees in a large greased and floured tube pan for 1 hour and 20 minutes, or until straw comes out clean. Ice with a butter frosting.

BUTTER FROSTING

1 stick margarine, softened
1 (1 pound) box powdered sugar
1 teaspoon vanilla
Milk

Cream margarine and vanilla. Beat in powdered sugar, adding milk to make desired spreading consistency.

MICHELE TAYLOR

PICNIC CARAMEL CAKE

2 cups cake flour, sifted
2 1/4 teaspoons baking powder
3/4 teaspoon salt
1 cup plus 2 tablespoons sugar
1/2 cup vegetable shortening
2/3 cup milk
1 teaspoon vanilla
2 eggs, unbeaten
1/2 cup nuts, finely chopped (toasted , if desired)

Line bottom of 9-inch square pan with paper; grease. Stir shortening just to soften. Sift in dry ingredients. Add milk and mix until all flour is dampened. Then beat 300 strokes by hand, or 2 minutes with mixer at low speed. Add eggs and nuts. Beat 150 strokes by hand, or 1 minute with mixer at low speed. Turn batter into pan. Bake at 350 degrees for 35 to 40 minutes. Cool cake in pan on rack for 5 minutes. Then loosen from sides, turn out, remove paper, and turn right-side up on rack to cool before frosting.

EASY CARAMEL FROSTING

1/2 cup butter
1 cup firmly packed brown sugar
1/4 cup milk
1 3/4 to 2 cups sifted powdered sugar

Melt butter. Add brown sugar and cook over low heat 2 minutes, stirring constantly. Add milk and continue to cook and stir until mixture comes to a boil. Remove from heat. Cool. Add powdered sugar gradually until of right consistency to spread.

THE TIMMERMANN SISTERS
GERONIMO, TEXAS

MILKY WAY CAKE

6 Milky Way candy bars
1 stick margarine
2 cups sugar
1 cup shortening
4 eggs
2 1/2 cups sifted flour
1/2 teaspoon soda
1 1/2 cups buttermilk
2 teaspoons vanilla

Combine and melt candy bars and margarine. Let cool. Cream sugar and shortening, then add eggs one at a time. Combine flour, soda and buttermilk alternately. Add candy mixture and vanilla. Bake in 3 greased and floured cake pans at 350 degrees for 30 minutes.

CHOCOLATE MARSHMALLOW CREAM ICING

2 1/2 cups sugar
1 small can evaporated milk
1 stick margarine
1 (6 ounce) package chocolate chips
1 pint jar marshmallow creme
1/2 teaspoon vanilla
1/2 cup pecans

Cook sugar, evaporated milk and margarine in saucepan for 5 minutes, stirring constantly, until melted. Add remainder of ingredients and blend. Spread between layers and on top of Milky Way Cake.

CARROT CAKE

2 cups flour
2 cups sugar
I teaspoon baking powder
I teaspoon salt
I teaspoon cinnamon
3 cups shredded carrots
I cup vegetable oil
4 eggs

Grease and flour 13x9x2-inch pan. In mixer combine oil and eggs; add sugar and beat. blend in dry ingredients which have been sifted together, then fold in carrots. Beat at medium speed for 2 minutes. Bake at 325 degrees for 50 to 60 minutes. Allow to cool before frosting with Cream Cheese Frosting.

CREAM CHEESE FROSTING

3 ounce package cream cheese
¼ cup butter
I teaspoon vanilla
2 cups sifted powdered sugar

Beat together cream cheese, butter and vanilla. Gradually add sifted powdered sugar and beat until smooth.

BUTTER PECAN COOKIES

1 cup butter (**NOT** margarine)
³/₄ cup sugar
2 cups flour
1 teaspoon soda
¹/₄ teaspoon salt
1 tablespoon dark corn syrup
1 cup chopped pecans

Cream butter, then gradually add sugar. Blend in syrup and pecans. Sift flour, soda and salt together, then add to creamed mixture; mix well. Shape into long rolls, wrap in waxed paper, and chill until firm. Slice thin, bake on greased cookie sheet at 350 degrees for 10 minutes or until lightly browned.

JODY HODGES

NUT BROWNIES

²/₃ cup butter
1 ¹/₂ cups sugar
2 eggs
1 cup sifted flour
¹/₂ cup cocoa
¹/₂ teaspoon salt
¹/₂ teaspoon baking powder
1 teaspoon vanilla
¹/₂ cup chopped nuts

Blend butter, sugar and eggs. Combine flour, baking powder and salt and mix well. Stir in vanilla and nuts. Spread in greased 8-inch square pan. Bake at 375 degrees for 25 to 30 minutes.

PAT TEPE

MRS. BLISS' BROWNIES

2 cups sugar
2 sticks melted butter or margarine
3 squares unsweetened chocolate
4 eggs
1 cup flour
1 small package or ³/₄ large package semi-sweet chocolate
chips (see instructions)
1 teaspoon vanilla
¹/₂ cup nuts (optional)

Melt butter and chocolate squares in saucepan. Let cool. Stir melted butter and chocolate into sugar. Add eggs, flour, chocolate chips, vanilla and nuts, in order listed. Bake in greased 9x13-inch pan at 350 degrees for 25 to 28 minutes. Cut while hot. If you use small package of chocolate chips, these are like brownies. If you use ³/₄ of a large package, these are like fudge brownies. I always use ³/₄ of a large package.

ROSALIE FILIPPONE

TANGY ORANGE COOKIES

These are very sweet, so make the balls small. Notice there is no baking involved.

1 stick butter or margarine, melted
1 pound box vanilla wafers, crushed
1 (6 ounce) can frozen orange juice, thawed
1 pound box powdered sugar, sifted
1 cup nuts
1 cup coconut

Mix sugar and orange juice, then add melted butter, wafers and nuts. Roll up cookies by teaspoons. Roll balls in coconut. Chill until ready to serve.

SAND TARTS

3 cups flour
5 heaping tablespoons powdered sugar
1 ¹/₂ cups butter (not margarine), melted and cooled
1 ¹/₂ tablespoons water
1 ¹/₂ tablespoons vanilla
1 ¹/₂ cups ground nuts

Sift flour and sugar together, add butter. Add water, vanilla and nuts. Mix well. Pinch off dough the size of a small egg and roll between the hands into a crescent shape. Bake in a slow 300 degree oven 45 minutes or until brown. Cool and roll in granulated sugar.

SNOWBALLS

These keep well in tins and make nice holiday gifts.

¹/₂ cup butter or margarine
3 tablespoons powdered sugar
1 cup sifted flour
1 cup ground pecans
Powdered sugar
1 teaspoon almond extract

Cream butter, almond extract and 3 tablespoons sugar until fluffy. Stir in flour gradually, then pecans until well blended. Chill several hours. Roll dough into marble-size balls. Bake in slow oven (250 degrees) for 20 minutes. Cool on cookie sheets 5 minutes. Roll in powdered sugar while still warm to coat.

I keep losing weight but it keeps finding me.

CHOCOLATE SNOWDROPS

This is a chocolate version of snowballs.

¹/₂ cup (1 stick) margarine
3 tablespoons powdered sugar
²/₃ cup sifted flour
¹/₃ cup dry cocoa mix (sugared mix)
1 cup nuts (almonds or pecans)

Cream margarine with 3 tablespoons powdered sugar. Stir in flour and cocoa mix, then chopped nuts. Chill until firm enough to handle. Roll dough a teaspoon at a time into marble-size balls. Place 2 inches apart on ungreased cookie sheets. Bake 20 minutes at 325 degrees. Remove while warm. Roll in powdered sugar. Cool completely on wire racks. Makes 4 dozen.

★

CINNAMON STICKS

My mother, Evelyn Mistrot Keys, made this simple and delicious cookie.

2 sticks butter or margarine
1 cup sugar
2 cups flour
1 teaspoon cinnamon
1 teaspoon vanilla
1 egg yolk
1 egg white, beaten until stiff
1 cup chopped nuts (optional)

Beat together butter, sugar, flour, cinnamon, vanilla and egg yolk. Press real thin in cookie sheet. Cover with beaten egg white. Sprinkle with nuts if desired. Bake 1 hour at 300 degrees. Cut while warm; let cool in pan.

FORGOTTEN COOKIES

3 egg whites (room temperature)
1 cup sugar
Dash of salt
1 cup chopped pecans
1 cup chocolate chips

Preheat oven to 350 degrees. Beat egg whites until frothy. Blend in sugar and salt, beating until firm. Add pecans and chocolate chips. Drop by teaspoon onto a foil-lined cookie sheet(s). Put cookies in oven. Cut oven off! Do not open oven for at least 8 hours or overnight.

PAT TEPE

PECAN CRISPIES

¹/₂ cup butter
6 tablespoons brown sugar
6 tablespoons sugar
1 egg
¹/₂ teaspoon vanilla
1¹/₄ cups sifted flour
1 teaspoon baking powder
¹/₄ teaspoon baking soda
¹/₄ teaspoon salt
1 cup chopped nuts

Cream butter and sugar until light and creamy. Beat in eggs and vanilla. Sift together dry ingredients. Blend into creamed mixture, and stir in nuts. Drop by teaspoon on ungreased cookie sheet. Bake at 375 degrees for about 10 minutes. Cool cookies before removing from pan.

PAT TEPE

BISQUICK BARS

This mixture makes a bar relatively like a brownie with the same consistency, but has a different taste. Keep tightly covered.

2 cups biscuit mix
1 pound box light brown sugar
4 eggs, well beaten
2 cups chopped pecans

Combine biscuit mix and brown sugar. Add to well beaten eggs. Then add chopped pecans. Grease and flour 13x9-inch pan. Pour into pan and bake at 325 degrees for 30 to 35 minutes. Remove from oven and let cool before cutting into bars.

BANANA SOFTIES

Just like banana nut bread, but a cookie.

$^2/_3$ cup shortening
1 cup firmly packed brown sugar
1 egg
1 teaspoon vanilla
1 $^3/_4$ cups flour
$^3/_4$ teaspoon salt
1 teaspoon baking powder
$^1/_4$ teaspoon soda
$^1/_4$ cup milk
1 cup oatmeal
$^3/_4$ cup mashed bananas
$^1/_2$ cup pecans

Beat shortening and sugar together until creamy. Add egg, vanilla and banana; beat well. Sift together flour, baking powder, salt and soda. Add to creamed mixture alternately with milk, mixing well. Stir in nuts and oats. Drop by teaspoonsful onto cookie sheets. Bake at 350 degrees for 12 minutes. Makes 5 dozen.

DARK FRUIT BARS

A glass of milk or cup of tea is a perfect partner for these scrumptious cookies.

¹/₂ **cup sweet butter**
¹/₂ **cup sugar**
¹/₂ **cup dark molasses**
1 egg
1 cup flour
¹/₂ **teaspoon salt**
¹/₂ **teaspoon cinnamon**
³/₄ **cup chopped walnuts**
¹/₄ **cup golden raisins**
¹/₂ **pound dates, pitted and chopped**

Cream butter with sugar and add molasses. Add egg and beat until light. Add flour sifted with salt and cinnamon, followed by walnuts, raisins and dates. Mix everything together, then pour into a well-greased 8-inch square cake pan. This is a very wet, sticky, lumpy dough so you will have to use your fingers to spread the dough to the corners of the pan. Bake in a 350 degree oven for 35 to 45 minutes. Cool thoroughly before cutting into squares.

An optimist laughs to forget;
a pessimist forgets to laugh.

MOTHER'S FRUIT COOKIES

To make the sour milk, add 1 teaspoon vinegar to 1 cup milk.

³/₄ cup margarine or butter
2 cups sugar
2 eggs
2 tablespoons sour milk
I teaspoon soda
Dash of salt
I teaspoon cinnamon
I teaspoon nutmeg
¹/₂ teaspoon cloves
2 ¹/₄ to 2 ¹/₂ cups flour
2 cups pecans, chopped
I cup raisins

Cream butter and sugar very well. Add eggs one at a time and beat. Add 1 teaspoon baking soda mixed in sour milk. Then sift dry ingredients together and add slowly. Last, add raisins and pecans. Drop onto greased cookie sheet and bake at 325 to 350 degrees. These cookies are best mixed by hand and when baked should rise and slightly fall again.

ELENORA KOHLENBERG

A house is who you are, not who you ought to be.
—Jill Robinson

FRUIT COCKTAIL COOKIES

*These are like little fruitcakes, but without the candied
fruits. They're especially nice for the holidays.*

1 can fruit cocktail
^{1}/$_2$ cup shortening
1 teaspoon butter flavoring
^{1}/$_2$ cup brown sugar
^{1}/$_4$ cup sugar
^{1}/$_2$ cup nuts
^{1}/$_2$ cup raisins
^{1}/$_2$ teaspoon vanilla
1 egg
2 cups flour
^{1}/$_2$ teaspoon baking powder
^{1}/$_2$ teaspoon soda
Dash salt
^{1}/$_2$ teaspoon cinnamon

Drain cocktail, save syrup. Cream butter (shortening); add vanilla,
egg, and butter flavoring. Beat well. Add sugars. Sift dry ingredients, add alternately with ^{1}/$_3$ cup syrup from cocktail. Stir in nuts,
raisins, spices and fruit cocktail. Drop by teaspoons on greased cookie
sheets. Bake at 375 degrees for 10 minutes.

CLARA MAE'S DATE SWIRL COOKIES

These cookies are very pretty and really good. They keep well.

$^1/_2$ **cup butter**
$^1/_2$ **cup brown sugar**
1 egg
2 cups flour
$^1/_2$ **teaspoon baking soda**
$^1/_2$ **cup sugar**
$^1/_4$ **teaspoon salt**
1 teaspoon vanilla

Cream butter and sugar, add egg. Stir in flour sifted with dry ingredients. Chill. Toss on floured board and roll out $^3/_8$-inch thick in rectangle shape. Spread date mixture thinly and roll up lengthwise in jelly roll. Chill. Slice $^3/_8$-inch thick and bake 10 minutes at 350 degrees.

FILLING

$^1/_2$ **pound chopped dates**
$^1/_4$ **cup nuts, ground**
Dash of salt
$^1/_4$ **cup brown sugar**
$^1/_3$ **cup water**

Cook together 5 minutes. Let cool while mixing dough.

CLARA MAE'S RAISIN COOKIES

*This is another good comfort food recipe. With a glass
of milk, you'll think you're 8 years old again.*

1 1/2 cups raisins
3/4 cup water
1 teaspoon baking soda
1 1/2 cups sugar
1 cup butter or shortening
2 eggs
3 1/2 cups flour
1 teaspoon salt
2 teaspoons cinnamon

Cook raisins in water until liquid is absorbed. Add baking soda.
Cream shortening (butter), add sugar and eggs. Beat well. Add sifted
dry ingredients and raisins. Mix into dough. Refrigerate 1 hour. Make
into balls. Flatten with fork. Bake at 375 degrees for 10 minutes.

★

LEMON BUTTER COOKIES

1 cup butter
2 1/2 cups flour
1 tablespoon lemon extract
1 cup sugar
1 tablespoon vanilla extract
1 large egg

Cream butter and sugar, add beaten egg. Add flour and extracts and
mix well. Make small balls, flatten slightly with your hands, and
bake on baking sheets at 350 degrees for 12 to 14 minutes.

MAKE COOKIES FROM ANY MIX!

Any cake mix
2 eggs
$1/2$ cup cooking oil

Mix cake mix, eggs and cooking oil. Drop by tablespoonsful on cookie sheet. Bake at 350 degrees for 10 minutes. Add any goodies you please; for example, raisins, nuts or chocolate chips.

BOB AND MARILYN KEYS

COWBOY COOKIES

This is a family favorite, and requested at all holiday functions!

1 cup sugar
1 teaspoon baking soda
2 cups rolled oats
1 cup shortening
$1/2$ teaspoon salt
1 teaspoon vanilla
1 cup brown sugar
$1/2$ teaspoon baking powder
1 (6 ounce) package chocolate chips
2 cups flour
2 eggs

Cream shortening and sugars; add eggs and continue beating until fluffy. Add flour, soda, salt, baking powder and vanilla. Mix until well-blended. Add rolled oats and chips (optional additions: raisins, nuts, coconut). Drop by teaspoon on cookie sheet about 2 inches apart. Bake 12 to 13 minutes at 350 degrees. Yield:about 7 dozen

JILL KNEUPER

GERMAN LOEP COOKIES

This is a dense, rather firm cookie that is good for dunking in coffee or milk.

3 cups white sugar
I cup water
I cup butter or margarine
I tablespoon cloves
I tablespoon cinnamon
I tablespoon nutmeg
I teaspoon baking soda
6 cups flour
2 tablespoons baking powder
2 cups whole pecans or large pecan pieces

In saucepan over medium heat, cook sugar, water, butter, cloves, cinnamon and nutmeg until mixture spins a thread. Let cool. Dissolve 1 teaspoon baking soda in a little warm water. Add to flour, baking powder and pecans. Add sugar and spice mixture and blend thoroughly. Pack in 8x8-inch pan. Cover and let stand in refrigerator for 8 days (yes, 8 days!). Cut in 2^1/$_2$-inch strips in pan. Lift out strips and cut in bars. Place on greased cookie sheet and bake at 325 to 350 degrees for 10 to 12 minutes. Watch carefully so that cookies don't get too brown.

ELENORA KOHLENBERG

Dull women have immaculate houses.

AUNT EMILIE'S ZIMMTSTERNE COOKIES
(Cinnamon Stars)

1 pound sugar
$1/2$ pound (2 sticks) butter
4 eggs
$1/8$ teaspoon cinnamon
2 teaspoons baking powder
2 cups flour
Ground pecans or almonds (optional)
Mixture of 1 part cinnamon to 4 parts sugar

Cream butter and sugar until light and fluffy. Add eggs one at a time, beating well after each addition. Combine flour, baking powder and cinnamon. Add to butter-sugar mixture; mix well. Add ground nuts, if desired; mix well. On lightly floured surface, roll $1/4$-inch thick. (If dough is too moist, gradually add flour.)Cut in shape of star. Place on greased cookie sheet. Sprinkle with cinnamon-sugar mixture. Bake in 350 degree oven for 20 minutes. Cool slightly; remove from pan.

THE TIMMERMANN SISTERS
GERONIMO, TEXAS

CARAMEL GRAHAM CRACKERS

24 cinnamon graham crackers
1 cup pecans, finely chopped
1 cup brown sugar, packed
$1/2$ cup butter
$1/2$ cup margarine

Line a baking sheet with foil. Cover with a layer of graham crackers. Mix butter, margarine and sugar in saucepan. Bring to a boil and cook for 2 minutes. Pour over crackers, sprinkle nuts on top, and bake at 350 degrees for 12 minutes. Cut into triangles.

MOLASSES COOKIES

$^3/_4$ **cup shortening**
1 cup sugar
$^1/_4$ **cup molasses**
1 egg
2 teaspoons baking powder
2 cups flour
$^1/_2$ **teaspoon cloves**
$^1/_2$ **teaspoon ginger**
$^1/_2$ **teaspoon cinnamon**
$^1/_2$ **teaspoon salt**

Melt shortening, add sugar, molasses and egg. Stir in dry ingredients. Mix until smooth. Chill in refrigerator. Form into balls with teaspoon. Bake at 375 degrees for 8 to 10 minutes. Makes 3 dozen.

★

GINGER COOKIES

$^2/_3$ **cup vegetable oil**
1 cup sugar
1 egg
4 tablespoons molasses
2 cups sifted flour
2 teaspoons soda
1/2 teaspoon salt
1 teaspoon cinnamon
1 teaspoon ginger
$^1/_4$ **cup sugar**

Mix oil with 1 cup sugar. Add egg and beat well. Stir in molasses. Add dry ingredients which have been sifted together. Shape into balls and roll in $^1/_4$ cup sugar. Place 3 inches apart on cookie sheets and bake 10 minutes at 350 degrees. Remove to wire racks to cool. Makes 5 dozen.

PUTSY'S MICROWAVE FUDGE

This was our Aunt Putsy Giles' recipe.

1 ¹/₂ cups sugar
¹/₃ cup cocoa
Dash salt
³/₄ cup milk
3 tablespoons butter
3 tablespoons crunchy peanut butter or ¹/₂ cup pecans

Mix sugar, cocoa, salt and milk in microwavable bowl. Cook mixture in microwave on high 4 minutes. Stir in butter and cook 7 minutes more. Stir and test a small amount in ice water. A soft ball that can be picked up with fingers should form. Add crunchy peanut butter or pecans. Stir until glossy and spread in buttered pan. Cut in squares to serve. Works every time!

BOB AND MARILYN KEYS

EVELYN'S PERFECT PRALINES

*This recipe came from our mother and mother-in-law,
who traditionally made pralines at holiday time.*

1 cup brown sugar
1 cup white sugar
1 teaspoon baking soda
1 cup buttermilk
¹/₈ teaspoon salt
2 tablespoons butter
2 ¹/₂ cups pecan halves

In a large, heavy saucepan combine the sugar, soda, buttermilk and salt. Cook over high heat for five minutes (210 degrees on candy thermometer), stirring constantly and scraping bottom of pan. Add butter and pecans. Continue stirring constantly and scraping bottom and sides of pan until soft ball stage (234 degrees). Remove from heat and cool slightly. Beat until thick and creamy. Drop by spoon onto waxed paper; let cool. Yield: 18 2-inch pralines.

BOB AND MARILYN KEYS

DIVINITY

This is a traditional Christmas candy at our house.

2 cups sugar
¹/₂ cup light corn syrup
¹/₂ cup water
¹/₈ teaspoon salt
2 egg whites
I teaspoon vanilla
I teaspoon powdered sugar
Chopped pecans

Mix sugar, corn syrup, water and salt in saucepan. Slowly bring to a boil, stirring until sugar dissolves. Cook to hard ball stage (260 degrees). Meanwhile, beat egg whites until stiff. Gradually pour hot syrup into egg whites, beating constantly. Beat until candy begins to hold its shape. Beat in vanilla and powdered sugar, then add pecans. Drop from teaspoon onto waxed paper. Let stand until firm. Store in airtight container.

BOB AND MARILYN KEYS

A balanced diet is a cookie in each hand.

ENGLISH TOFFEE

5 tablespoons water
2 sticks real butter
1 cup sugar
2 Hershey chocolate bars
2 cups whole pecans

Combine water, butter and sugar in saucepan over medium heat. Cook to 310 degrees. Spread pecans on foil on cookie sheet in oval shape. Pour cooked ingredients over pecans. Place broken chocolate bars over top of candy; let melt and spread evenly with back of spoon. Sprinkle chopped pecans over chocolate. Let cool 1 hour and break into pieces.

RONALD SCHRIEWER

CHRISTMAS MINTS

$^1/_3$ cup light Karo syrup
1 teaspoon peppermint extract
$^1/_4$ cup butter, softened
$^1/_2$ teaspoon salt
4$^3/_4$ cups sifted confectioners sugar
Red and green food coloring

Blend Karo syrup, butter, peppermint extract, salt and powdered sugar; mix with spoon and then with your hands until smooth and mixed thoroughly. Divide into thirds; add one drop of red food coloring to one third and one drop of green food coloring to one third. Leave the other third white. Shape into small balls, flatten with fork on waxed paper and let dry for several hours. There is no cooking involved with this recipe.

SAUCES, SANDWICHES & SPECIAL TREATS

Antique store fixtures loaded down with jars of fresh-picked produce, salsas, jams and jellies line the shelves of the Gruene General Store, along with handmade crockery to decorate the kitchen. Memories of the past abound as you gaze at the old tins and hard-to-find items throughout the store.

SUN-DRIED TOMATO PESTO

Keep this on hand in your fridge. Mix it into butter for picnics—
as a last minute topping for soups—to toss it into hot pasta—to pour over
cream cheese for parties. Make some and let your creativity flow!

¹/₂ cup sun-dried tomatoes, softened in hot water, and drained
³/₄ cup walnuts, toasted
I cup fresh basil
³/₄ cup olive oil
³/₄ cup Parmesan cheese, grated
6 garlic cloves
I teaspoon pepper, freshly ground
Salt to taste

Measure all ingredients into food processor. Process until ingredients are thoroughly chopped. Taste for salt. Refrigerate or freeze. Makes 1 ¹/₂ cups.

CYNTHIA PEDREGON
PEACH TREE TEA ROOM
FREDERICKSBURG, TEXAS

CRANBERRY ORANGE RELISH

This is so easy. Buy and freeze fresh cranberries in the fall so you'll
have them on hand all year. I make this year-round and serve with
broiled or baked chicken breasts. The canned stuff can't hold a candle
to freshly made cranberry sauce. It also makes nice holiday gifts.

I (16 ounce) package fresh cranberries
2 cups sugar
I teaspoon shredded orange peel
I ¹/₂ cups orange juice

Combine ingredients and bring to a boil. Boil gently 10 minutes. (Watch carefully for boil-over). Cool. Store covered in refrigerator. Makes 4 cups.

BLENDER MAYONNAISE

$^1/_4$ to $^1/_3$ cup olive oil, then fill remainder of cup with corn oil
I egg
$^1/_4$ teaspoon salt
$^1/_4$ teaspoon dry mustard
2 tablespoons fresh lemon juice

Pour $^1/_3$ cup mixed oil into blender container. Add eggs and spices. Blend on high for 2 seconds, turn blender down as low as it will go and gradually add remainder of oil. Blend on high for 2 seconds. Store covered in refrigerator.

HOMEMADE MAYONNAISE

I egg
I teaspoon mustard
I teaspoon salt
I teaspoon sugar
Dash of pepper
2 tablespoons lemon juice or vinegar
2 cups oil

Beat egg, mustard, salt, sugar, pepper and lemon juice very thoroughly. Keep beating as you add oil. Keep refrigerated.

ELENORA KOHLENBERG

LIME-CILANTRO MAYONNAISE

This is good on any kind of sauteed fish as a substitute for tartar sauce, or as a dressing on top of sliced tomatoes. It adds an interesting Southwestern touch.

1 ½ cups mayonnaise (low-fat is okay)
1 ½ ounces lime juice
1 ounce cilantro, chopped

Combine all ingredients in a bowl; refrigerate.

BLENDER HOLLANDAISE

Easy to make, and delicious on fresh asparagus or Eggs Benedict.

3 egg yolks
2 ½ tablespoons fresh lemon juice
Parsley
Pepper
½ cup butter at room temperature
¼ cup boiling water

Place all ingredients except water in blender. Blend at medium speed and then with blender running, gradually pour in boiling water. Run for 1 minute on medium. Pour into small saucepan and heat, stirring constantly, over hot water until consistency of custard.

MARCHAND DE VIN SAUCE

This is a delicious sauce; traditionally it is served with roast beef, but it can also dress up a hamburger steak and is good over mashed potatoes.

¹/₂ cup butter
¹/₃ cup finely chopped mushrooms
¹/₂ cup minced ham
¹/₃ cup finely chopped shallots
¹/₂ cup finely chopped onion
5 cloves garlic, minced or pressed
2 tablespoons flour
¹/₂ teaspoon salt
¹/₈ teaspoon pepper
Dash of cayenne
³/₄ cup beef stock or consomme
¹/₂ cup dry red wine

In a small heavy saucepan, melt butter and saute mushrooms, ham, shallots, onion and garlic. When onion is golden, add flour, salt, pepper and cayenne. Brown well, about 7 to 10 minutes. Blend in the stock and wine; cover, and simmer over very low heat 35 to 45 minutes until reduced to 2 cups.

BILL BARRY'S BARBECUE SAUCE

1 stick margarine
1 cup vinegar
1 cup water
1 (4 ounce) bottle Lea & Perrins Worcestershire Sauce
1 bottle A-1 Sauce
1 lemon
Dash of Tabasco
Salt and pepper

Boil all ingredients together, then simmer for a few minutes. This will keep indefinitely in the refrigerator.

ELIZABETH BARRY

CHILI SAUCE

Chili sauce is good with black-eyed peas or pinto beans. This is my grandmother's recipe.

6 quarts ripe tomatoes (quarter to measure)
1 ¹/₂ cups chopped onions
4 large or 6 small green peppers
2 or 3 hot peppers
3 pints mild vinegar
4 cups sugar
2 tablespoons salt
2 tablespoons cinnamon
1 ¹/₂ teaspoons cloves
1 teaspoon nutmeg

Chop all vegetables fairly small. Combine all and cook in a large pan until thick. Seal in jars while hot. Cool and store in refrigerator.

MOREDADDY'S PIMIENTO CHEESE

Once you've tried this, you'll never go back to the store-bought version again. Makes great sandwiches; also use to stuff celery for a veggie plate.

1 ¼ **pounds sharp cheddar cheese, grated**
2 **(4 ounce) jars diced pimientos, drained**
1 **(8 ounce) jar Pace Picante sauce**
Freshly ground pepper
3 **tablespoons mayonnaise**

Combine cheese, pimientos and picante sauce. Add pepper to taste. Add mayonnaise and blend thoroughly. Store in refrigerator. This is quite hot; use less picante sauce for a milder mixture. Makes 1 quart.

CARROT SANDWICHES

Great quick snack or light lunch!

1 **(8 ounce) package cream cheese**
1 **large carrot, grated**
1 **cup chopped pecans**
1 **teaspoon garlic salt**
1 **tablespoon mayonnaise**
1 **loaf health nut bread**

Blend together cream cheese, grated carrot, chopped pecans, garlic salt and mayonnaise. Spread on health nut bread for sandwich.

ANNA BODE
JEFFERSON GENERAL STORE
JEFFERSON, TEXAS

CHOPPED HAM SANDWICHES

These are absolutely delicious, and great for a luncheon!

1 small onion, minced
1 tablespoon poppy seed
3 tablespoons prepared mustard
1 teaspoon Worcestershire sauce
1/2 pound margarine, softened
1 pound Swiss cheese, sliced
1 1/2 pounds chopped ham
24 sandwich buns or Kaiser rolls

Mix onion, poppy seed, mustard, Worcestershire and margarine and spread on both sides of buns. Fill with ham and 1 slice of Swiss cheese. Wrap in foil and put in oven about 15 minutes at 300 to 325 degrees.

TERRY ZENGLER

★

OLD FASHIONED SALT CUCUMBERS

This pickle recipe is from the Hartmann family, one of the original German settlers in New Braunfels.

6 medium to large whole cucumbers
1 quart cold water
1/4 cup vinegar
1/3 cup salt
2 fresh dill sprigs
2 grape leaves

Pack cucumbers in stoneware pan or crock. Mix salt, water, vinegar, grape leaves and dill, pouring mixture over cucumbers. Cover and refrigerate. After one week, remove cucumbers from mixture and serve.

ADELINE MAE HARTMANN

GRANDMOTHER'S DILL PICKLES

Cucumbers
Fresh dill
1 clove garlic
1 grape leaf
1 hot pepper (optional)

Brine:
1 quart water
1 cup 90 grain vinegar
1/4 cup pickling salt (no iodine)

Wash cucumbers by hand and cut off stem ends. Put fresh dill, garlic, grape leaf and pepper in large canning jar. Pack cucumbers tightly. Make brine with water, vinegar, and pickling salt. Bring brine to rolling boil, pour over cucumbers and seal. Place jars in hot water bath for 10 minutes.

ELEANOR COLDEWAY

SPICED FRUIT

1 (30 ounce) can peach, apricot, or pear halves or pineapple chunks
1 cup honey
¹/₂ cup vinegar
¹/₂ cup Aspen Mulling Spices

Place drained fruit in a 1 quart jar. Heat honey, vinegar and Aspen Mulling Spices to boiling. Pour over fruit; cool. Cover and refrigerate at least 8 hours.

ASPEN MULLING SPICES
ASPEN, COLORADO

CORN MUSH

*This is a real old-fashioned country dish which can
be used as a breakfast cereal or supper dish.*

1 cup corn meal, regular or stone ground
3 cups milk
¹/₂ cup sugar
Salt to taste

Cook cornmeal and 1 cup of milk over low heat until it thickens;
add another cup of milk, then add ¹/₂ cup of sugar and last cup of
milk, stirring frequently. This will thicken and when cool will be
much thicker. Cook for at least 1 hour. This is equal to 4 breakfast
servings, with milk added, or can be used as a side dish.

Elenora Kohlenberg

COWBOY GRAVY

Serve with biscuits or, for a surprise twist, ladle gravy over hamburgers.

Lard or bacon drippings (or substitute vegetable oil)
Flour
Water
Onion, chopped (optional)

Cover bottom of heavy skillet with equal parts lard or bacon drippings, and flour. Cook over medium heat, stirring constantly, until
roux is medium-brown in color. Add onion, if desired. Add enough
water to make gravy of desired thickness, stirring constantly. Cook
for 5 minutes.

The Timmermann Sisters
Geronimo, Texas

SUMMER SAUSAGE

1 cup water
2 tablespoons Morton's Tender quick tenderizer
1 teaspoon black peppercorns
¹/₄ teaspoon garlic salt
¹/₄ teaspoon garlic powder
2 teaspoons mustard seed
2 teaspoons liquid smoke
1 teaspoon crushed, dried red peppers
2 pounds ground meat (lean)

Combine first eight ingredients. Add ground meat. With hands, mix all together. Be certain ingredients are well-distributed and thoroughly mixed. Shape into two rolls about 2 to 2-¹/₂ inches in diameter. Wrap each roll securely in aluminum foil, making sure shiny side is to the inside. Crimp foil on each end so meat is not exposed. Put rolls in plastic bag and refrigerate for 2 to 3 days. Take rolls out of plastic bag. With fork, punch two holes in each end of foil (top and bottom). Place on a broiler pan and bake at 350 degrees for 1-¹/₂ hours. Cool. Refrigerate. Slice to serve. The longer it lasts, the better it gets!

THE TIMMERMANN SISTERS
GERONIMO, TEXAS

The real proof of a woman's courtesy is to have an ailment just like the other woman is describing and not tell her about it.

HOMEMADE NOODLES

*This recipe is nearly 100 years old! Dry noodles freeze well. Cut pasta
may also be wrapped in plastic wrap and refrigerated up to 24 hours.
The thinner and fresher the pasta, the shorter the cooking time.*

2 eggs
2 to 3 tablespoons milk
1 ¹/₂ to 2 cups flour

Combine eggs and milk (measure milk by filling ¹/₂ an egg shell).
Beat well. Add enough flour to make a stiff dough. Roll very thin,
about ¹/₈-inch thick, on floured surface. Let stand about 20 minutes
or until partially dry. Roll up loosely; slice ¹/₄-inch wide; unroll,
spread out and let dry (about 2 hours). Drop dry noodles into boiling soup or boiling, salted water and cook uncovered 10 to 20 minutes, depending on thickness of noodles.

THE TIMMERMANN SISTERS
GERONIMO, TEXAS

★

HOMEMADE SOAP

15 gallons water
20 pounds fats
4 boxes lye

Combine ingredients in large iron kettle. Boil until it thickens and
spins a thread when stirred (will take 3 hours or longer). Let this
cool overnight. It will thicken and can be cut in squares or blocks
the next morning. An old saw is ideal for cutting. Place squares on
board to dry.

ELENORA KOHLENBERG

ONION SKIN EASTER EGGS

This Old World technique makes stunning eggs.

Dry skins from yellow onions
Eggs (brown eggs turn a deeper, richer color in this process)
Vegetable oil

Prior to the Easter Season, save the yellow-brown dry onion skins from your purchased onions in an open air bag. When ready to dye eggs, place onion skins in a large glass or enamel pot to a depth of about 2 inches. Place eggs in a single layer on the bed of onion skins and add about two quarts of water. Cover. Bring to a boil and barely simmer 15 to 18 minutes on low heat. Gently remove eggs to a bowl under cool running water. Place cooled eggs on paper towels and dry. Polish each egg with a towel moistened in vegetable oil. The eggs are colorfast and will not stain fingers or linens. Refrigerate.

For fanciful decoration on the eggs, place a fresh sprig of green leaf such as carrot or parsley on a small square of old, clean nylon hosiery. Place egg on leaf and carefully pull the corners of the nylon up and over the egg. Tightly twist the four corners of the nylon and secure with thread wrapped around the twist about 8 times. Tie thread in a knot to hold fast. Then boil egg as directed above.

THE TIMMERMANN SISTERS
GERONIMO, TEXAS

INDEX

CONTRIBUTORS

Aspen Mulling Spices - Aspen, Colorado

Barry, Elizabeth - New Braunfels, Texas

Blue Dog Inn - New Braunfels, Texas

Bode, Anna - Jefferson General Store, Jefferson, Texas

Brown, Margaret - New Braunfels, Texas

Chilek, Concetta - New Braunfels, Texas

Clagett, Jack - Austin, Texas

Coldeway, Eleanor - New Braunfels, Texas

Cone, Bill & Connie - New Braunfels, Texas

Crocker, Beth - New Braunfels, Texas

Dickerson, Carmen Lucia - Houston, Texas

Filippone, Rosalie - Houston, Texas

Fischer, Julia A., Fischer & Weiser Specialty Foods - Fredricksburg, Texas

Frase, Pat - Georgetown, Texas

Gristmill Restaurant - Gruene, Texas

Gruene, Kyle & Ethelene - Gruene, Texas

Hartmann, Adeline Mae - New Braunfels, Texas

Hodges, Jody - Aledo, Texas

Howell, Karen - New Braunfels, Texas

Hughes, Daphne - Copperas Cove, Texas

Huisache Grill - New Braunfels, Texas

Hunter, Tammy - New Braunfels, Texas

Hutchins, Una - Grand Prairie, Texas

Jardine's Texas Foods - Buda, Texas

Keys, Bob & Marilyn - Katy, Texas

Keys, George - Honolulu, Hawaii

Kneuper, Jill - Junction City, Kansas

Kohlenberg, Elenora - New Braunfels, Texas

Macredie, Janie - Guadalupe Pit Smoked Meat Company, Gruene, Texas

McCaskill, Bill and Sharon - Gruene Mansion Inn, Gruene, Texas

McGilvray, Anne - New Braunfels, Texas

McIlhenny Company - Tabasco Brand Products

Melton, Garlanda - Houston, Texas

Miles, Billie - Gruene Homestead Inn, Gruene, Texas

Nealeigh, Cynthia Hartmann - New Braunfels, Texas

Noble, Angela D. - Seguin, Texas

Olympic Lights Bed & Breakfast, Friday Harbor, Washington

Pedregon, Cynthia - Peach Tree Tea Room, Fredricksburg, Texas

Quinn, Melanie - Somers, Connecticut

Salt Grass Steakhouse - Houston, Dallas, and San Antonio, Texas

Schriewer, Ronnie - Geronimo, Texas

Shannon, Shari - Hunter Junction, Gruene, Texas

Strasser, Fran - New Braunfels, Texas

Taylor, Michele - New Braunfels, Texas

Tepe, Pat - New Braunfels, Texas

Timmerman Sisters - Geronimo, Texas

Wolfmueller, Jon & Sandy - Pampell's Drugstore, Kerrville, Texas

Zengler, Marilyn - New Braunfels, Texas

Zengler, Terry - New Braunfels, Texas

GRUENE GENERAL STORE COOKBOOK
Hughes Interests
5325 River Oaks Drive
New Braunfels, TX 78132

Please send me _____ copies of the *Gruene General Store Cookbook* @ $16.95 each _____

Texas residents add sales tax 1.40 each _____

Postage and handling 3.50 each _____

TOTAL $ _____

Enclosed is my check or money order in the amount of _____

Drivers License # _____ State _____

Name _____

Address _____

City _____ State _____ Zip _____

Telephone _____

GRUENE GENERAL STORE COOKBOOK
Hughes Interests
5325 River Oaks Drive
New Braunfels, TX 78132

Please send me _____ copies of the *Gruene General Store Cookbook* @ $16.95 each _____

Texas residents add sales tax 1.40 each _____

Postage and handling 3.50 each _____

TOTAL $ _____

Enclosed is my check or money order in the amount of _____

Drivers License # _____ State _____

Name _____

Address _____

City _____ State _____ Zip _____

Telephone _____